What The Stars Reveal About The Men In Your Life

Edited by Thelma White

Published by
Melvin Powers
WILSHIRE BOOK COMPANY
12015 Sherman Road
No. Hollywood, California 91605
Telephone: (213) 875-1711

Printed by

HAL LEIGHTON PRINTING COMPANY
P.O. Box 3952
North Hollywood, California 91605
Telephone: (213) 983-1105

Printed in the United States of America
Library of Congress Catalog Card Number: 79-56313
ISBN 0-87980-378-9

contents

There Is A Reason For It All / 5
What's It All About? / 9
Aries / 11
Taurus / 21
Gemini / 3
Cancer / 43
Leo / 53
Virgo / 63
Libra / 73
Scorpio / 83
Sagittarius / 93
Capricorn / 101
Aquarius / 113
Pisces / 123
What You've Always Wanted
To Know About Horoscopes / 135

tHERE IS a REASON foR It all

Throughout the centuries man has looked to the stars. In wonder, in confusion, and in hope, he has gazed into the heavens to find answers to his earthly questions. And he found them. Using the orderly patterns of the planets, a map or chart could be created. Each individual had their specific chart and certain aspects of their lives related to known patterns. In ancient Egypt, horoscopes were cast for kings and pharoahs. For many centuries the Chinese never made an important decision without seeking celestial advice. The heavens were carefully plotted to find the most auspicious date to marry, to bury a loved one, to build a home or take a trip.

The events in your life don't just happen. There is a reason, a moment in time, a conjunction of planets that makes one encounter different from another, that makes you respond the way you do.

You are a single woman at a party and you spot an interesting man across the room. He smiles and comes over to you. Immediately you are mutually attracted. You feel as if you had known each other for years.

The usual artificial conversation gambits are suddenly unnecessary. His eyes crinkle when he laughs and you like him. There is a magic in the air around him and an indefinable sense of camaraderie between you both. You laugh together and the conversation flows along easily without either of you trying. The evening suddenly becomes a total high for you and for him. Other people smile at you both together because they sense your happiness. There are moments of laughter, understanding, and companionable silences. It is RIGHT. You both glow and shine. Is this love? Sex? What is the magic spark that drew you together, that kept you together through the evening?

Very likely it was a happy combination of two compatible signs, well aspected and responding to each other because of lunar influences. At a different time and place, the meeting could turn out differently, so take advantage of the right moment.

You are trying to present a sales program you have planned very carefully. It is important for your future goals that the meeting be exactly right. The person to whom you are making the presentation sits silently. How are you coming across? You don't seem to be making the impact you desired. You know there are many aspects of the program that are profitable for both of you and yet he or she just sits there. What is going on behind that mask of politeness? How do you spark the interest, how can you motivate that person so important to you?

If you knew the birth sign of your prospective client you could have set up the meeting for a time when all the signs were favorable.

Your husband has moods that change for no reason. Perhaps he takes forever to make up his mind and you may be quick and mercurial in your decisions. Or maybe he drives you crazy by darting off in new directions by whim or fancy. Is it because he's a man? Does the all important male ego make him unfathomable? If you know his sign, you will know why he reacts as he does.

You arrive at work one morning and your boss has suddenly become suspicious of everyone around him. He questions the motives of even his trusted associates. Why?

Your child never seems to be able to make up his mind. Your employee, whom you have known for years, has fits of the glooms that can react unfavorably on your customers. Why?

What motivates people to strive for love, power and money? Why can't some people stand success? Can you stand success? Do you deliberately shoot yourself down after you have achieved a long sought goal? Why do some people attract love, power and money and others seem always to have sudden, unexpected misfortunes?

The stars, the planets, the sun and the moon all bring their influence to bear on our lives. You can change your life, make it richer and more meaningful by understanding these elements and using them to your advantage. If you know that your Virgo man, whether husband, lover or friend, will always be skeptical, his "show me" attitude won't dismay you. Accept the stolid Taurus as he is, he won't change, so don't delude yourself into thinking his love for you will make him different, or that you will be able to change him.

Your new neighbor is charming and fun and yet the next time you meet, seems determined to cause you trouble for no definable reason.

Your parents decide to split after twenty-five years of marriage. There seemed to be the average amount of loving and fighting and making up, but you sense they really are going to separate permanently. You are baffled.

What makes people react as they do? Why do you feel a sudden kinship with someone you have just met and, in contrast, another person you hardly know annoys you and makes you irritable? Why is that sales presentation going badly? What has gotten into your husband, your parents, your boss? Why has a president of the United States pulled his success down into tatters and disgraced himself?

This book is written to help you understand that fascinating, yet frustrating enigma, why the people who are important to you react as they do. You can learn to deal with them to your advantage. We all need power, love and success to survive happily. This book will show you how best to utilize the knowledge you have to attain these goals.

You will learn for example that Cancer people do have strange moods when the moon is full and can be expected to be silent and withdrawn. You will understand that Cancers need the security of a loving home and plenty of food around them to make them happy. You will realize why love is more important than food to Leos. You will suddenly see why that Gemini man can be two different people, as if he were twins; he is twins. The dreamy eyed Piscean is only being himself when he seems to see right through you and knows your thoughts without being told.

The Scorpio who suddenly lashes out at you for a wrong you did to him unintentionally three years nine months and three days ago, will no longer surprise you. You will learn that Scorpios don't forget wrongs or kindnesses. You will understand your small Arian son who can't make up his mind to eat his meat or vegetables first and is almost immobilized there in his highchair. You will be able to sense what is motivating your Capricorn, who, now that he has accumulated a fortune, spends so much time on committees for the Historical Society. He actually looks younger every day, younger in features and outlook, than when he was a youth. He was too busy amassing that money to enjoy himself, but now that he's achieved his goal, he's having the time of his life.

The Virgo man you meet at the cocktail party who is so immaculately dressed and counts your drinks will seem less mystifying. Cleanliness is all important to his happiness and he can't help counting.

Your Sagittarian lover with his wide-eyed view of life will always answer you frankly when you ask, "How do you like this dress?" He will no longer distress you with his bluntness. Who else would be so honest and, after all, you did ask him.

The Aquarian who wears the granny dress and exists in some future time warp but does visit back here with her friends now and then will not be so puzzling.

You will learn how the rising sign, the planet which was rising at the time of your birth, can modify personality. You will learn how the moon affects everyone of us. Most important, however, is the sun sign. It denotes whether a person is a Leo, Aquarian, or Libra or any of the other signs. This knowledge can and will help you understand your lover, your friends, your husband, your boss, your co-worker, your child.

You are probably already aware of your own sun sign and you have, no doubt, furtively read the astrology column in the newspaper. You have sensed there is a reason behind this seemingly puzzling life. When you know your own sign and realize the influences it has on your own life you can proceed to learning about those dearest to you, or those you want to make dearest. When you have all the answers, there's no place to go but onward to success.

what's it all about?

Once a year the Earth revolves around the Sun in a rather wobbly, elliptical orbit. The other planets, the Moon, Venus, Mercury, Jupiter, Mars, Saturn, Uranus, Neptune and Pluto also revolve around the Sun in their own orbits. This circle around the Sun in which all these planets move is called the Zodiac.

The circle around the Sun which these planets make is between fifteen and eighteen degrees wide and has twelve subdivisions, or Signs, and each contain thirty degrees of longitude. The way the Earth revolves around the Sun takes a year to complete its orbit. Thus, the Sun passes through one of the twelve signs of the Zodiac each and every month. This explains which Sun sign you are born under. If the Sun was passing through the sign of Aries at the time of your birth, for example, your Sun sign is Aries. If the Sun was passing through the sign of Leo at the time of your birth, you are born under the Sun sign of Leo and so on.

At the exact moment of your birth, wherever you were born, in America, Australia, Europe, Asia or wherever, all of the planets mentioned above were in certain specific places in the heavens. When an astrologer computes exactly where these planets were at the time of your birth it becomes a map or a chart and is called a horoscope.

WHAT DOES A HOROSCOPE LOOK LIKE?

The horoscope is a map of the heavenly bodies for a specific time from a specific moment on earth. It is a circle divided into twelve equidistant segments of thirty degrees each, like the spokes of a wheel. The lines which divide these segments are called cusps. The areas within the segments are called "houses," twelve in all. Each house denotes a definite sphere of influence in your life. Imagine you were holding this chart up to the sky at night. It is exactly opposite from a geographical map of the land because you are looking upward at the stars.

The first house is always at nine o'clock and the chart is read counterclockwise. As an example, if you were born on August 10, 1934, your Sun sign would be Leo. The signs never change their order; Taurus always follows Aries, Sagittarius always follows Scorpio.

To get an accurate horoscope, you must know the exact time of your birth. If you were born an hour later or earlier than you believe, you could have an entirely different rising sign.

If you want to cast charts you will need reference books telling you the location of the signs in the twelve houses, the placement of the Moon, and the rising sign. There are two kinds of charts, solar and natal. A good astrologer can, of course, cast your own chart for you if you are interested.

The following descriptions of the sun signs and their influence on an individual are drawn in rather broad terms. In stating how a Tauraus will react in certain situations, for instance, means that this is what you can usually expect from the Taurus, or your Leo or your Virgo. In order to pin down specific responses it would be necessary to know a lot more about him. At what exact hour was he born? What year? What day? Where? The clues you get in the following chapters should answer any questions you might have.

ARIES

March 21-April 19

HIS ABILITY TO LOVE A WOMAN

Under the sign of the ram, Aries the conquerer is fascinated by challenging women. He likes to think he is going to sweep you off your feet and he isn't too subtle about it. He thrives on competition but he always has to be first. If you are dating another man he will be even more interested. He is impatient to find out all your secrets and will ask very direct questions. Perversely he is often captured by the cool, feminine slightly mysterious woman who can keep him dangling without making him angry.

Once he has his eye on you, he will be a flattering and exciting date. Expect to participate in all sorts of outdoor sports with him. In fact, if you don't like ski slopes and tennis courts, you had better come up with something else to hold his interest. He is usually bursting with ideas and he needs an audience for them. He dearly loves to talk and he likes a companion who can discuss all sorts of ideas with him. He is interested in his ambitions, the stock market, what is wrong with the country, and most of all, his plans. Bone up on current events so you can be knowledgeable and stimulating. This man thrives on communication.

He also thrives on dominating you sexually, and he has some fascinating ideas about that, too. He is the conqueror, in bed as well as everywhere else. When he gets down to serious sex he has a remarkable staying power and fairly orthodox ideas. He attacks sex with the same zest with which he plays tennis or skiis.

This man is not attracted to coy, cute women. They make him restless and impatient. He has a pretty well conceived idea of the girl he wants for a wife. Beauty, cleverness and devotion win his heart and once he makes up his mind that you have what he wants, pow! This man can be pretty overwhelming. His ruler is Mars, which represents passion, desire, energy, assertiveness, courage and initiative. Mars is also the God of war. He has been known to drive highstrung girls to complete destruction.

Your Arian has the fearlessness of a child, with the urge to experience everything for himself. He rushes headlong in an unwavering line to his objective. Then he repeats the same process toward the next objective. He may not take time to think, to grow and to develop.

He is a fighter and fights for causes, good ones, if he can find them. He is a pioneer and a trailblazer and he always has an ideal equal to the situation.

His creative urge is so strong that if he does not encourage it he is apt to cut himself off from life. Sometimes he is so impulsive he doesn't stop to think and he can fail because he doesn't take time to make careful plans. He has a tendency to let his talents drive him.

RELATIVES

He is kind and generous with his relatives. He likes to feel that he is part of a big family but he isn't too interested in listening to their problems. He loves family reunions and celebrations. If he is able, he will help them financially.

MONEY AND CAREER

Your Arian wants the affluent life but sometimes he stays with a job that offers security rather than growth. Security means a great deal to him. If he loses his job for one reason or another it is hard for him to find another. This is not because he is limited in ability but because he finds it difficult to take chances. His worst failing is his propensity to get himself into a deadend job while others with half his ability are promoted over his head.

He will be very loyal to his employer and often will acquire influential friends in the upper echelon of his company. He tends to attract people who are the leaders of the community. When he really enjoys his work and can use his creative ability he will be an outstanding success.

Some Arians are more successful working with tangibles such as machinery or services. This shows the practical side of his nature.

An Arian has the ability to inspire and lead others, but he usually doesn't make a very good executive. He tends to be unable to delegate authority and tries to handle all the details himself. His main strength lies in planning and conceiving ideas.

The creative fields claim many Arians. Your Arian may be a musician, writer, commercial artist, advertising layout worker, actor or dancer. He may be a salesman but sometimes he will be just too impatient to be tolerant of his customer's fallibilities. If he happens to be a doctor or engineer, he will be very successful, for here he can use his ability to think for himself to the fullest. As a teacher he will present his ideas in an interesting and novel way and may be voted the most popular teacher on the campus.

Like so many successful people he is highly sexed. He can transmit personal magnetism, which is after all, sexual energy. You will feel it in his voice and the aura of his personality. He probably will have a keen sense of humor and enjoy rather obscure jokes.

He can be careless about spending and sometimes, acquires great debts. He needs someone who can help him save and plan for the future.

HEALTH AND DIET

He is a very strong vital man. If he does become ill and must be hospitalized his room will be filled with as many visitors as the doctor will allow.

FRIENDS AND SOCIAL LIFE

He loves to entertain interesting and stimulating people in his own home. He makes friends easily and keeps them for years. His friends feel optimistic and confident with him. Often they seek him out to speak for them because he is so articulate. He will have friends on many levels, athletes, artists, business tycoons, all of whom share his drive and intensity.

CLOTHES HE LIKES TO SEE YOU WEAR

Bright red pants, gold chains and all kinds of jewelry interest him. Have some colorful sports outfits ready to go, he won't give you much notice and he will always arrive ahead of time for your date. Be prepared for some spur of the moment plan that could be enormous fun. A weekend trip to the training camp of a friend or a tailgate picnic at an off road race. It may sound weird, but he'll make it an enjoyable event.

FOODS THAT GRATIFY HIM

Your Arian will like meat and potato dishes but he is not too interested in vegetables and fruits. He likes exotic foreign foods and unusual dishes of any kind. He is so dynamic he doesn't need to drink much to enjoy a party and often doesn't drink at all. You might serve an after dinner drink to top off the meal. Some Arians don't even drink coffee and prefer the more relaxing cup of tea. If you do serve him tea, try some of the flavored or spiced kinds.

Here is a sample menu for your Aries friend and a few good pals so he can have some stimulating conversation. A small group is suggested. He does not like big stand-up cocktail parties where he never gets a chance to engage in discussions with people. He has so many interests and he does love to show off.

Pate with Crackers
Caesar Salad
Chicken Kiev
Fried Rice
Blueberry Muffins and Honey
Chocolate Mousse
After Dinner Drink you know he likes

WHAT KIND OF HUSBAND WILL HE BE?

If you like your Arian well enough to marry him, make him think that he is quite extraordinary. He really is. He is so articulate and charming that even when he is angry he is hard to resist. Of all the signs, he believes most in the direct approach.

He likes to rule the home. It may take him awhile to learn to compromise but he will always be fair and just with you. He sees you as an equal. You will never have to wonder what he is thinking and the two of you should communicate very well. In fact, conversation will be a major part of married life. He loves to talk, to ask, to discover. Be as honest and direct with him as he is with you; he just doesn't understand devious women.

He will probably be faithful to you, but he may indulge in a mild affair just to see if the old charm is still there. He will then return to you determined to let bygones be bygones. He does not intend to let any affair break up his marriage.

He dislikes rudeness and vulgarity of all kinds.

Your Arian will be up and about his many projects by six in the morning and will bring you coffee in bed so he can talk to you. Make sure you are never too busy to listen to him and encourage him to discuss his plans with you. Your marriage will never be dull with this man as long as you can communicate with him.

WHAT KIND OF FATHER WILL HE BE?

He takes pride in children and will encouage them to be creative. His enthusiasm and zest for life will be transmitted to them. He will have innovative ideas about their education, for example, he may not encourage them to go on to higher learning; he may instead urge them to go into some sort of technical training. He will leave the matter of their religious training to you.

ARIAN CO-WORKERS

Arians usually don't have too much of a problem getting hired. At the initial interview they are prepared to tell an employer all about his company and thus convince him that they want to work there because the employer is so creative and has such a great product. They are capable of overwhelming him with so much energy and optimism that they get hired before the employer knows what has hit him. Once in the company, the Aries employee is rather like a rocket. If he starts out in a position where he can use his creativity and initiative he will repay the employer ten times over with his zeal and brilliance. He can institute ideas that save time and money and he does it with such style and originality his employer will wonder why he didn't find him earlier.

If, however, the employee finds himself in a dull, routine job he will become restless very soon. When this happens he reacts by becoming careless and may start goofing off. When the ram gets bored his shortcomings outweigh his virtues. He hates to punch a time clock. If possible, the employer should allow him greater flexibility with his hours—

let him come to work on the new popular flex time and he will be there as long as necessary to get the work out. He may arrive at six in the morning and not come in until ten the next morning; but he also is not averse to staying until midnight to polish off a new presentation or whatever he is working on at the moment. He loves to have some leeway, and challenge is his meat and drink. Any new creative idea he has will be fleshed out no matter what the hour. Ideas buzz around in his head at all hours. He may keep a pad and pencil by his bed to jot down thoughts he has at night.

If he has the latitude to use his ideas and develop them he will be a very valuable employee. He is a great promoter and will represent the company probably better than any other sign. He will be enthusiastic about his firm to his friends, golf partners, anyone he meets, because he is a natural salesman. He has the gift of gab of Gemini and the charm of Leo. He must be assured that he is appreciated, though, or he will slack off and look for greener pastures. He is such an idealist that he can't believe that his boss would just take for granted all those projects he put over single handedly. He also can't conceive of failure, the company's or his own. An Aries woman, hired for dull hum-drum jobs in a banking institution talked the management into letting her edit and publish a newspaper about the bank's various activities in the community. This was an instant success. It also, happily, got her promoted to a more interesting position with the bank. Soon, she began to combine the publication of the newspaper with some public relations work which also proved successful for herself and the bank. In an unexplained move, the upper echelon in the bank decided to drop the newspaper and the public relations work and demoted her back to her dull, hum-drum job. After a very short time she quit. The next thing her friends heard was that she had gone to work for another financial institution and later was named Woman of the Year. She is a typical Arian.

Bosses usually don't have to fire Arians. If they feel they are being ineffective they quit. Also, typically, rams rely on their hunches. They seem to have an uncanny ability to sense what is going on around them and are seldom fooled. They have the gift of knowing what to do when and are usually quite lucky. They never suffer a defeat for long. To most Arians a defeat is turned into a greater opportunity. Of them you could say if they get a lemon, they will turn it into lemonade.

THE ARIES BOSS

This man makes up his mind fast; he will hire you fast, point out your mistakes fast and will always have to be RIGHT. He himself has so much energy he cannot identify with lazy employees and he will expect you to work as hard as he does and to be as concerned with the progress of the company as he. This is no spot for you if you are not prepared to work hard, overtime if necessary, and present innovative ideas as often as you sensibly can. He is a human dynamo and he will expect you to be as enthusiastic as he is or he simply will not be able to work with you. He is an "idea man" and will probably be fascinating to work with, you will never know what he is going to come up with next. You may find that he is so interesting that you will look forward to going to work for him, even if the slot you happen to fill isn't terribly important. Imagine the Aries boss who teaches a class in his spare time, collects antiques and sells them, all this along with running a successful company. All the more reason, he feels, to have employees who have the ability to keep the shop running while he is off involved in his other projects.

On the other hand, this man will listen sympathetically if one of his employees has a personal problem which requires time off, for whatever reason. He understands that sometimes his employees need some recreation and recovery time, not too often mind you, but now and then he gives his permission. Just be careful and don't abuse the R & R or he will let you know about it in very scathing terms. He does not like people to take advantage of him. He has a way of delivering his tongue lashing that leaves no room for argument. He simply tells you, briefly and concisely, and then gets onto some other more pleasant business. He may give you a second or even a third chance, but that's about it. There is a curious detached "me first" attitude with this man, or woman, and you must never forget this. He always has to be first, just as he always has to be right. Whatever you do, don't get involved in an argument with him. He does not like people to disagree with him. In fact this is about the quickest way for you to get fired. There is a deeper more obtuse reason for this quirk in his character. Secretly he doubts his abilities to run the company as he thinks it should be run, and your criticism will strike a very tender spot. For all his verve, panache and style, he really is a rather sensitive man, and much more vulnerable than you might think. He loves praise but he is very quick to spot insincere flattery. If you can praise him honestly when he just pulled off a clever maneuver, he will love it. Nothing he does has value to him unless other people know about it and praise him. He likes money, of course, and will work hard for it, but the recognition of his peers means even more. He simply has to be noticed. He can be downright petty and mean if he thinks he isn't being properly appreciated. You may not have an indication of why he is being quiet and withdrawn because he is so good at hiding his hurts. However, he doesn't retreat into these moods for long. If you are intuitive enough to give him the necessary ego petting he so badly needs, he will bounce back with his old verve and swagger. Back to the Aries boss. His employees kid about his "hyper" moods and his depressed moods, but they are careful to do it with kindness. You never know what kind of a mood he will be in, but it runs from a high to a low. He is an interesting individual to work for if you don't allow yourself to be continually upset by his changing manner. He is so creative and inventive it is easy to overlook his wide mood swings.

He needs other people more than he ever will admit to anyone, but he also has tremendous strengths and will go it alone if necessary. When he is in the midst of a creative project he may work night and day. Another Aries boss wrote a book on psychology in three months, all while holding down his regular company duties. He wrote it after work, sometimes staying up all night. It was so controversial and presented such unorthodox ideas that he hasn't yet been able to get it published but no doubt he will eventually, probably when he finds a publisher who is an Aries, or perhaps an Aquarian. This Aries boss is now off and running simultaneously on three other pet projects.

Aries bosses, or Aries people, for that matter, live in the present. They are not concerned with the past or the future and they do not worry or fret. If something doesn't work out they spend no energy stewing about what what can't be helped. The big world is out there and they have plenty of new ideas to carry out. Aries people sometimes have so much energy and ideas that they wear other people to a frazzle. Leos and Pisceans often find themselves exhausted trying to keep up with an Arian. Leos have energy too, but after a while they like to retreat and let the world go its way. Pisceans simply can't understand all that thrashing around. Scorpios do understand his drive and are equally energetic but less idealistic and motivated. Sometimes Scorpios succeed over Arians because they aren't as handicapped by conscience.

One thing you must remember about your Aries boss is that he will have no patience with you if you are out sick frequently. He himself never gives in to illness unless he is on his deathbed. He can be really ill in the morning and somehow psyche himself out to the point that he will show up for work by noon hale and hearty. He will expect his employees to do the same.

If you like excitement and chaos and an office where there is always something going on you will love working for an Aries. There will never be a dull moment. Give him lots of praise when he needs, don't ever get sick and you won't have to worry about getting sacked. He will repay loyalty with loyalty and be generous with the bonus, too. Take the details off his hands and be prepared to enjoy his success with him.

TAURUS
April 20-May 20

HIS ABILITY TO LOVE A WOMAN

The Taurus man has a very strong sexual nature. He likes to touch and to be touched. He adores his creature comforts, evenings at home with you in a plush and relaxed setting. He really is rather earthy. He likes "substantial" women and if you are really thin he will delight in fattening you up. You can forget your diet when you are with him. This man is sensual and responds to feelings. He usually dates only one girl at a time and may demand that you drop all your other involvements. The first time he dates you, it may seem he has known you forever. Very likely he has watched you from a distance before making his move and has decided that you might make a good wife. He really likes married life best and tends to act more like a husband than a date.

Taurus is the sign of bankers and financiers. Financial chaos drives him crazy. He will not lend a sympathetic ear to your tales of overdrawn checking accounts and unpaid bills. He can be bluntly critical, for your own good of course. He is a plodder and a bit slow to react. If you provoke him he can be a veritable thunderstorm of fury. Sometimes he flies into a rage because he doesn't know what else to do but feels he should do something.

He is trustworthy and he will depend upon you to do what you said you would do when you said you would do it. He will arrive promptly for your date and he expects the same from you. If he finds he can't depend upon you he will quickly become disenchanted. Give the impression that you are well organized and can manage the details of your life situation very capably and you will win his admiration. He is not much at whispering sweet nothings and if he does compliment you it may not be in the way you handle financial matters. He will show you that he loves you by his steady dependability but flowery phrases are difficult for him. He can also be very stubborn. If you hurt his feelings he may forgive you but he won't forget.

He likes to be complimented on his figure. If he has a mini paunch tell him you like substantial men. Should you marry him he will expect you to help him watch his diet, but more about that later.

Your Taurean is more calculating than impulsive and his reactions are slower than some of the other signs. He is friendly and companionable and not easily caught off balance. He is not so calculating as the Capricorn man but among other things he will carefully consider your financial aspects. Once he has made his decision that you are the one he truly loves, he will leave no stone unturned to get you.

Oddly enough, he may promise you more than he actually means to give you. This seems to be rather common among Taureans, a trait winning them some unpopularity.

Venus is the ruling planet of Taurus and your Taurean is affectionate and sentimental although he is so quiet and reserved he doesn't always seem to be an outwardly affectionate man. He enjoys art and music and likes the finer things in life.

You may meet him at the opera, a museum or at your broker's office. In fact, he may be your broker. If he gives you a tip on a stock to buy and you follow his advice he may offer to make your loss up if it goes down. He is very sincere in all his dealings so don't play games with him. If he decides you are not to be trusted he will become very angry. If you have a misunderstanding with him try to get it straightened out before he has time to brood. If he comes up with the wrong conclusions you will have great difficulty inducing him to change his mind. Taurus is an obstinate sign. He cannot be driven but he can be lead with affection and love.

RELATIVES

Before he marries you, Taurus will be a bit casual about his own relatives. He is primarily concerned with his home and you. After you marry him he may help you with your needy relatives because he feels responsible, but he won't be too happy about it. If he feels your relatives became needy through their own improvidence he may become very stubborn about offering any kind of help and this could create some difficulty in your domestic life. Taurus likes to entertain his relatives once in a while for family celebrations but he is not as sentimental as some of the other signs.

MONEY AND CAREER

Your Taurean is born a trader. By the age of eight, he probably acquired the most marbles in his class, and time has only sharpened his business acumen. What he loses on small deals he makes up on big ones. In whatever field he finds himself, he is very quick to see opportunities that exist. In fact he may be juggling several businesses at once. In a large corporation, he sees employees as one big family and he as father to them all. He does expect loyalty and his orders must be followed to the letter. If he is an employee he will carefully consider his obligations to his employer and be extremely conscientious in carrying out his duties.

He is a born organizer and he likes detail work. Sometimes he gets so bogged down in the details of a hum-drum type job that he does not advance.

As a salesman he can be very successful but he has to be convinced of the merits of the product or service or he cannot sell. He would usually sell articles of practical value, not luxury items.

He is a outstanding success in handling other people's money. He is so honest and "old shoe" that people believe in him and trust him. He may be a financial consultant, stock broker or a consultant engineer, a corporation lawyer or administrator of estates for a banking firm. He sometimes takes all responsibility too seriously and tends to worry that he has not done his job as well as he could.

If he has his own business it will probably be in a rather conservative field, he does not take too readily to new and untried products.

He will do well as a restaurant manager, hotel manager, caretaker or gardner.

As a rule, your Taurean will not become impatient for immediate success but will pursue his goal steadily.

Your Taurean and his money will seldom be parted. Taurus is the sign of bankers and millionaires. They are, of course, not all bankers and millionaires but you won't find them in unemployment benefit lines either. That's because he builds slowly and surely and early on decides how he is going to earn his living. Whatever he decides to do will be his one vocation. He doesn't go flitting about the economic jungle like Aquarias trying to find himself. He found himself years ago and he has no time for that silliness. He thinks its ridiculous as one Taurean friend put it, "to spend all that time thrashing around looking for the gold at the end of the rainbow." He knows he has to work for what he gets.

HEALTH AND DIET

Taurus likes meals that stick to his ribs and he has a better developed sense of smell than any other sign of the zodiac. He will remember the tasty food you served him more for its aroma than for its flavor. With Italian or Mexican food he likes a good red wine. Make sure you have a pleasant, tranquil atmosphere during dinner. Noise and excitement upset his stomach.

The areas prone to infection and accident are the throat, neck, legs, ankles, reproductive organs, the back and spinal areas. Sore throats usually follow colds and hang on longer than one would expect. He will probably be plagued increasingly by overweight problems as he grows older. The Taurean love of good food and drink causes problems with his circulation and some Taureans even suffer from the malady which victimized wealthy lords and nobles in the middle ages, gout. Once the bull realizes he can lose his robust good health by overeating and drinking he can rapidly reverse his pattern of life. He is nothing if not realistic, though it will be harder for him to diet than for some of the air and water signs. Don't forget he is an earth sign, remember the land. Earth signs are much more fixed in outlook than air and water signs and Taureans tend to have tunnel vision. Air signs are Gemini, Libra, Aquarius. Water signs are Cancer, Scorpio, Pisces. The other earth signs are Virgo and Capricon. Do you see some of the similarity in characteristics in Capricorn and Taurus? Taurus and Virgo?

The bull is healthiest and most at home in the country where he has room for plenty of exercise. His system seems to demand it. Getting him to realize this is something else again. He is STUBBORN!

Your Taurean will have a healthy appetite and he may sometimes overeat. He has good recuperative powers if he does become ill. His ruling planet affects his neck and shoulders.

FRIENDS AND SOCIAL LIFE

Your Taurean is naturally friendly by nature but he can be intolerant even with his old friends. He is a great believer in tradition and the establishment. You won't find a Taurus marching in protests. He is not relaxed or easy going with his friends and he may tend to manage them.

CLOTHES HE LIKES TO SEE YOU WEAR

This man is a trifle old fashioned. He likes his women to be well dressed in rather conservative, well-cut clothes. Since he is a romantic at heart you can wear very feminine outfits, such as big floppy hats and sheer, pastel summer dresses. He will give you plenty of warning about the type of affair he has planned for your date so you will know what to wear.

HOW TO ENTERTAIN YOUR TAUREAN

When a Taurean courts you he really courts you. He seldom arrives at your door empty handed. Your Valentine box of candy will be huge and sentimental. When you entertain him at home make it a really old fashioned apple pie and roast beef type of dinner. He doesn't like very dainty, insubstantial food. Potatoes and gravy are a sure-fire pleaser. This kind of dinner will remind him of mom and security and that's where it really is for him, security and the home. Here is a suggestion for that special meal for your Taurus:

Green Salad or Carrot Salad
Roast Beef
Oven, Pot, or Crockpot
Carrots, Potatoes, Onions in a
Rich Brown Gravy Sauce
Homemade Rolls
or Bread
Apple Pie with Cheddar Cheese

Music puts him in a romantic mood, have some soothing records or tapes ready to play softly in the background. Color sends his senses soaring. All shades of blue are favorites of Taurus. Shades of rose and pink are good. Typical of a Taurean is one who has recently blossomed out in clothes that are shades of violet and purple. He watched men's styles changing over the years and just decided to brighten up his wardrobe. He only made these changes recently; he didn't want to rush into anything.

For hospitality your Taurean will love, try having a musical evening. Invite someone who plays the guitar for instance. If you play the piano, invite a few musical friends over. Ones who like to gather around and sing. Your Taurean will probably have a melodious voice and will love to show that he has a few talents, that is, he can sing. He does like music and although he may be a little shy about joining in, an evening like this will let him shine. He will remember you as a gracious hostess who made him feel very special.

FOODS THAT GRATIFY HIM

Although he enjoys Mexican or Italian foods, avoid fancy sauces and most seafoods when you plan to entertain him. Big, juicy steaks, potatoes and gravy, fresh salad and apple pie will please him and make him think you are a good cook. If you serve drinks have rather substantial snacks ready to serve along with them. He may like a short nap after dinner.

WHAT KIND OF HUSBAND WILL HE BE?

Becuase he is ruled by Venus he has the qualities that makes for a happy marriage. He will settle down in the routine of the home and become a very devoted husband. He has wanted to be a husband all his life. To him, marriage is the only way to live and he gladly accepts his responsibilities in married life. He does not regret being married and he does not make raunchy jokes about husbands verses wives.

He will expect you to prepare delicious meals and he may put on weight unless you diplomatically modify his tastes for rich foods. He does like to eat so take care or you may end up with a roly-poly husband.

Your Taurean will be happier at home than almost anywhere else so make sure it is well managed. He will see that you have all the labor saving appliances that you need and he will keep them in good repair.

Outside interests will probably have something to do with art and music. He will expect you to go to concerts and museums with him. He will enjoy helping you decorate your home so that it is beautiful and artistic.

Stubborness often extends to a Taurean's family life. Even if he has made a poor choice in marriage and his spouse is making him acutely miserable he finds it extremely difficult to extricate himself. To him, marriage is the only way to live. His loyalty to home and family often passes understanding and he will patiently try any means he can think of to improve the situation, or failing that, simply live with it. Two examples of Taureans, one a man, one a woman, were caught in truly miserable marriages. The woman would probably never have divorced her philandering husband, unhappy as she was. Fortunately, he divorced her. The male Taurean, married twenty years and a father of three children, patiently lived with a hypochondriac wife who refused to cook, clean or perform any household tasks. She simply dropped out. The Taurus husband and children did everything for her until she abruptly solved the problem by moving out and leaving him to deal with the household. Both Taureans, happily, did not brood for long on their misfortunes. They are now contentedly married to other spouses. Brooding is not a popular pastime for the bull. They cope well with a bad situation but they will get off the world when things get too hectic, and wait for matters to stabilize. Once divorced they tend to remarry easily.

Taureans especially enjoy being hospitable to people in their homes. His home will probably be in the country if he can possibly afford it. Taurus has an affinity for the land which spells security to him. Sometimes this extends to his occupation but more about that later. The land is important to the bull.

Taureans have a great appreciation for comedy, particularly the broad pie in the face musical hall variety. Taurus humor is warm and earthy and they fail to catch subtleties that are evident to Aquarius. They are delightful story tellers in the style of Andy Griffith. Did I say they are usually a bit old fashioned?

WHAT KIND OF FATHER WILL HE BE?

He will naturally expect to have children and will shower them with his attentions. He will see that they have every advantage he can give them. He will have high ideals for them. In short, he will delight in his role as father and protector. If they do not turn out as well as he hoped, he will accept their right to live as they see fit. He will offer financial help as long as they need it. He will be interested in school activities and may even serve on the school board or in PTA. He will be very conscientious toward his children. They will recall their childhood with Papa Taurus as the head of the household which was overflowing with love and warmth. He is patient and sympathetic. He will love boys and girls alike, although he will think it is important to have a son to carry on the family name. He will delight in his little girls and spoil them. He will set high standards for his children and teach them to respect property, their elders, and authority. He will teach them to enjoy music, but hard rock will drive him right up the wall, although he may let it go in one ear and out the other until he realizes what he is actually listening to. That may not be enough to upset the equilibrium of the bull, but if he is grumpy, tired and out of sorts, and he has repeatedly told his children to cool the rock music when he is home, look out. That may trigger one of those rare occasions when the bull simply erupts in furious anger. He doesn't blow up often, but when he does, it is frightening.

Most of the time when he is home with his family, the home will be filled with good music, beauty and peace and he will be the proudest papa in the block.

TAUREAN CO-WORKERS

If you happen to work in a real estate office you may be surprised to discover how many Taureans are lurking thereabouts. The land, remember? Although he may not be very verbal, he is happy as can be showing prospective clients through houses, and he actually does more showing than telling. Somehow this lack of hard sell, combined and obvious enthusiasm, impresses his clients. They sense his honesty. If they have any questions he will attempt to answer them candidly and if he doesn't know he won't hesitate to say so.

If you find him in another kind of business office he will probably be the individual who has most of the responsibility in his particular area. He enjoys building his little empire brick by brick. If he sees he is in a dead end job he will move on to another empire, brick by patient brick. Wherever he is working he will be a dependable employee and will not resent taking orders. He has great respect for authority and feels if the boss is paying him to work, he will work to please the boss. That doesn't mean he can be pushed around, though. If you watch his face while others try to pull this trick you will notice a sort of tongue in cheek attitude. This serves to humor those who try to drive him. He will, if pushed too far, react in several ways. One, a childish pout, or two, an explosion. After the explosion there may be a period of ominous quiet. He's thinking it over. If he decides he can't live with the situation he will quietly leave. He will not return for another try. If he decides to go, that is the last his boss will see of him. When he once finds an occupation, a pasture, that feels right to him, the bull will probably remain there a lifetime. Taureans usually manage to accumulate quite a bit of security either in the lower echelons or the management sphere.

You can recognize female Taureans by the rather limpid bovine look in her large eyes. She will probably be a good dancer, love music and have a natural sense of rhythm. She will move gracefully.

The male Taurean will be built like the bull with a heavy muscular neck and chest and a lock of hair resembling the forelock of the bull. Whether tall or short the body is well proportioned. Many Taureans have naturally curly hair. They do not give the impression of frailty. Moving slowly and deliberately, their feet seem to grow out of the ground. As mentioned before, he can become angry. Change that to more like destructive. One Taurean who worked in an office in the county courthouse absolutely did not, underlined, believe in astrology. However, he was so typically Taurean it was almost laughable. He loved music, not the rock and roll variety, was tall, had a heavy muscular chest and neck and his hair was sandy and naturally curly. A lock was usually hanging down the middle of his forehead. To anyone's recollection, he only hurried once, when a marshal, attempting to make an arrest, was himself attacked by his prisoner who outweighed him by fifty pounds. The marshall had succeeded in getting handcuffs on his prisoner but a scuffle ensued and he obviously needed help. The Taurean took in the situation at a glance, rushed to the aid of the marshal and bodily hauled the prisoner into a cell. That was five years ago, he hasn't hurried since, he hasn't seen the need to hurry. His nickname is "the terrible teddy bear."

Typically, this Taurean is stubborn. In fact, he can plant his feet, fold his arms and become the Taurean people describe in astrology books. In short, when his mind is made up he is immovable. His opinions are also set in stone and he is not averse to defending them. In his case, he may have a touch of Gemini because he is a very verbal and erudite man, which is not true of all Taureans.

The female Taurean is a pearl beyond price. She is pleasant, has a low modulated voice, and makes the greatest executive secretary. Typical is a charming gal who has been a legal secretary for the same boss for the past twenty years. If she left him his practice would literally fall apart, he depends on her so. Lady Taureans don't get rattled in emergencies. Other office workers seek them out when they get in a bind. While at work they will join in the office coffee session but will make sure they don't overstay the alloted time. They like people and enjoy the give and take of office life.

In addition, they don't watch the clock. They feel obligated to give the best they can to their job and willingly work overtime. Often they work for years in the same office. They always have their eyes on what really spells happiness, that is, a home and a husband. Like the male Taurean, married is the only way to live.

When the lady Taurus is discussing business matters with a man she can be rather tough and her conversation sounds more like that of a man than a woman. Her views are not flighty, she is not given to gossip and she is well informed about current events. When she settles on a man she has probably checked him out pretty thoroughly and if he happens to work in your office you can watch him on his way up. This is not to imply that she isn't feminine. She spends time and money on her personal appearance. Despite competence and mental sagacity, she is first and last a woman. She is not inclined to leave deep intellectual pursuits to the men. Even though she would rather be at the home, the Taurean wife will willingly go to work to help her husband achieve his goals. She has a good head for figures and easily manages the household accounts.

THE TAURUS BOSS

Your Taurus boss likes his employees to look attractive. He himself most likely wears expensive clothes, but he may be inclined to be a bit careless. He does most things "by the numbers." He operates pretty much on a schedule and has very definite habit patterns. Coffee at the same time each day, his desk organized just so. Incidentally, don't sit at his desk or use his personal possessions without express permission becaue it really upsets him.

You might make points with this boss by bringing him some special goodies to go with his coffee, such as some of your homemade cookies or light-as-a-feather croissants. He does like good food, and he also likes to be fussed over, very tactfully of course. Taureans like to eat, and they are inclined to equate food with security, much as do Cancers.

Your Taurus boss has some very definite ideas as to how he wants his business to be run. Don't make the mistake of changing any of the routines he has already set up. If you really think you have a worthwhile idea that would effect savings in time and increase profits you must use extreme tact in making the suggestion. Remember, Taurus can be led but never driven. If you think before you act you can win him over. Once he sees that you do have solid, practical business acumen, he will respect you. He is in business to make money, money not for money's sake, but for the luxuries it will bring him and his family. If he feels you are an honest, trustworthy employee who does have some good ideas, and if you can tolerate his fatherly stick-in-the-mud manner, you can look forward to a steady job. Taurus doesn't like to upset his schedules. If for no other reason than it is a hassle to fire people and hire others, he isn't quick to replace employees. However, if he thinks you have really been untrustworthy and haven't learned by experience, he won't hesitate to fire you. Taurus doesn't mind employees being rather slow to learn (he can be rather slow himself) and he will be very patient. He probably won't criticize you for some time letting you learn by experience, but then suddenly he will decide that you are either (a) really a dum-dum and will never learn, or (b) not to be trusted. If he arrives at either of these conclusions you have had it. Just remember, don't push him too far. When he makes up his own mind he rarely changes it. He won't indulge in shouting, screaming, verbal abuse, fire you, and then cool off and invite you back the next morning as a Gemini might. He doesn't like noisy arguments and is really quite gentle. Just don't go around waving the red flag of defiance, dishonesty or incompetency and all will be peaceful. He admires competent people, women especially, and will probably brag about you to others. He may not compliment you directly, but he might say something like "you'll do." That's high praise and you now have a steady job and a dependable boss.

GEMINI

May 21-June 20

HIS ABILITY TO LOVE A WOMAN

Gemini is the sign of the twins. He is really two people, both of them childlike. In love he is enthusiastic and convincing. One night he may keep you up talking till all hours, just to prove to you that he is not only interested in sex. The next night he may call you to say he is coming right over because he just has to see you. This night, he does not want to talk at all.

He is intrigued by variety—in your dress, your home, your hairdo and your conversation. Keep him guessing. He hates routine. Suggest spur of the moment jaunts, the more novel the better. When you take an egg out of the refrigerator for breakfast in the morning, ask him if he is alert, then toss it to him.

This man has a very analytical mind and can be difficult to understand. He will have a tendency to read between the lines and sometimes misconstrue what you say. He might have a cool, calculating tendency to observe you from afar, just to see what makes you tick. If he thinks he has you figured out, beware. The fascination will be over and he may flit

33

off to the next and the next. He is continually searching for his ideal woman. If you want to hold his attention let him think of you as a sexy, charming and stimulating companion. If he likes to discuss his business, read up on it so you can ask intelligent questions; however, don't try to be a know-it-all. He loves intelligent discussion and has a mind like a steel trap. A Gemini can be great fun, if you can keep up with him! Don't ever expect to win an argument with him, you can't. He can be totally convincing and he can also be a charming liar. Don't ask him where he was last night, let him guess where you were.

There is an effervescence, a lightness, in the quick and graceful movements of Geminis. They sometimes remind you of a hummingbird, a dancer, or a clown. The hair can be either light or dark, or even streaked. Both sexes usually have high foreheads and the men seem to lose their hair sooner than do other signs. Maybe all that mental activity has something to do with it. There are brown-eyed Geminis, but most of them have twinkling blue or hazel eyes that seem to dart here and there. Their alert, busy eyes are usually a clue to their sign, and you may notice their eyes before you realize you are looking at a Gemini. They never rest their eyes on an object for more than a few seconds. They are often pale, but they do tan beautifully, from the beach in the summer or the ski slopes in the winter. Most of them speak very rapidly, but sometimes their minds are working faster than their speech. Remember John Kennedy and his press conferences? Like all Geminis he had a sharp, perceptive sense of humor and thought very fast on his feet. One felt that he really enjoyed his verbal sparring with the press.

If you know your Gemini well at all you will probably notice with irritation a common habit they share. He may suggest an outing or a trip and then remember that he has a few errands to do first. You agree to go off with him and wind up sitting in the car while he flits around here and there. He is always "going to be right back." His right back can turn into hours. Somehow he always finds something or someone to investigate.

A Gemini friend can nearly drive you up the wall. Like other Geminis they seem to have an obscure compulsion to disguise their real thoughts and motives. They really are two people, so typical of this sign. He could be a tremendous salesman and literally sell the proverbial Eskimo the you-know-what. He can twist his prospective customers around his finger and they won't know what has hit them until he has dashed off with a stack of orders for goods they had no intention of buying. When he returns later to check with them and finds large stacks of merchandise unsold, he can somehow convince them they can still sell it and he then spends time showing them how. He might also have a rather unlovely personal trait. With his friends, he seems to have a genius for spotting their Achilles heel or the skeletons in their family closets and is not loath to rattle those bones if he thinks it to his advantage. There is not any particular hostility in these actions—his friends soon realize this is a sort of compulsion. Being always on the offensive, he has to win, and to do so he must have the upper hand. Perhaps because his mind is so keen and sharp, life in general becomes a game to him.

Mercury, as you know, rules Gemini. It also rules writing. Geminis are able to write well and can string words together so successfully they often work at advertising agencies, magazines and in television. They do not, as a general rule, write personal letters. Neither do they write autobiographies. There seems to be a strong hesitancy about putting their personal thoughts down on paper. They know they probably will change their minds the next day. The typical Gemini will put off answering his personal correspondence for weeks. He will probably end up calling long distance if he is really pressured. Geminis are also notoriously reluctant to commit themselves to anyone or anything and their attorney doesn't have to tell them "don't put it in writing." They already know this instinctively.

With a good ear to linguistics, foreign languages usually come easily for Geminis. They can also mimic an accent and can be hilarious story tellers.

A Gemini isn't usually long on patience. He may keep you waiting but he resents being kept waiting himself. This is a quirk you will have to learn to live with. He also lacks persistence and patience, unless he has a rising sign of Taurus or perhaps Capricorn. He can be very secretive and share his secrets with only one other person, his twin self. He often overlooks the happiness in his own backyard for something elusive over the rainbow, and makes the same mistakes over and over. He is continually searching for an ideal. This search can go on for his entire lifetime.

Your Gemini may be like a little boy who never really grows up. He likes and admires women and can't help showing it. Because he is so charming and spontaneous he may promise a woman more than he really means to deliver. Throughout his courtship there may be a pixie-like quality that is truly engaging. You may want to clasp him to your breast like the waif he is. The next minute you may be looking for a blunt instrument. Keep your cool with this man and be prepared for the unexpected. His one consistency is his inconsistency.

He needs physical affection; don't just tell him you love him, show him. Compliment him whenever you can. He simply blooms when you tell him how much you admire him. He isn't as sure of himself as he seems.

The Libra man likes to express his views and the Aquarius man likes to stay with a particular subject and explore its various aspects. The Gemini man can jump from topic to topic with the speed of light. He may make a statement on a particular point and immediately be off on some other subject.

He can change his mind at a moment's notice and you can often wind up visiting three or four places during an evening out. Spend some of your spare time checking out new places you think he might like and surprise him occasionally with a suggestion.

Your Gemini loves to talk with people. He can strike up a conversation with the cocktail waitress or a perfect stranger he meets on the street. He can be holding a conversation with you and be watching someone else across the street or across the room. He is rather intellectual in his approach to women. He is more of a talker than a doer. Sometimes he seems to be looking for a loving, indulgent mother figure. Everyday he goes forth, wide-eyed and eager, expecting to find life exciting and worthwhile. He is not snobbish and believes everyone is his brother or sister. He is unafraid and expects to find only good in others.

RELATIVES

Your Gemini will be much more fond of his relatives than his friends. He will show them a steady, enduring love and this relationship will help to balance his life. If your relatives are interesting people he will seek their company and they will become his family also.

MONEY AND CAREER

A Gemini man is a naturally shrewd trader and shows his talent early in life. He is quick to see where he can turn circumstances to his own advantage. He seems to know what to do and when, this springs from a sixth sense. Sometimes she outsmarts himself, but he recovers quickly. As a salesman, buyer, copy writer, owner of an automobile agency, he is tops. He does best when he can compete with others.

In the medical field, he would be an asset in any sort of research work. Because he is inclined to be abrupt, irritating patients could drive him up the wall.

In the field of law he is at his best as a trial lawyer. He thinks on his feet. He is a talented speaker and actor. Law offers an arena he loves. If he does go into law he could easily go on to a political career.

You may meet him as an office manager, a job he will like as long as he can supervise others who do the detail work.

Because he is so versatile and creative he may be a writer, artist, composer, actor, all of which he combines with some hard-headed business sense. Briefly, he can be a success in any business or profession which offers variety.

Your Gemini is a skilled conversationalist and may be a fluent linguist. He has a natural gift for words and understands their uses. In fact, the Gemini man is gifted enough to accomplish almost anything he sets out to do, and the reason he doesn't always succeed is rather complex. Because he has a dual nature, he is two people and is constantly being pulled in two directions. He has great difficulty making choices because he can always see something good on either side. He will sometimes start the day with all sorts of great resolutions and at the end of the day become quite depressed when he realizes he hasn't accomplished very much. A badly aspected Gemini seldom finishes anything he starts because he loses interest.

Another reason for your Gemini man not achieving what he is capable of achieving is his propensity to bargain with his integrity. He can easily persuade himself that it is in his own best interests to do some particular thing he wants to do, regardless of whether it hurts himself or someone else. You can, if you are a clever woman, help him in this area. He will talk everything over with you and if you love each other, your efforts will bring deeply satisfying rewards to both of you.

HEALTH AND DIET

High strung and sensitive, he seems to be continually on the go. He may smoke more than he should. He may, early in life, drink more than is good for him, but his instinct for self preservation usually comes to the fore and saves him from overindulgence. It is difficult for him to rest and when he is ill, his recovery may be slower than the other zodiacal signs. Once he has decided he is well, he will be on the go with all his old vim and vigor.

Mercurial Geminians need all the rest they can get. It is hard for them to get enough sleep and they frequently suffer from insomnia. The reason is because they have such agile, busy minds its hard for them to turn off their thinking processes long enough to go to sleep. They need lots of fresh, unpolluted air and lots of sunshine to keep them healthy. They are so high strung that nervous exhaustion is always just around the corner. They are subject to accidents and infections of the shoulders, arms, hands, and fingers. The lungs may be weak, and also the intestines. Not a few Geminis suffer from ulcers. If they neglect their health they may have problems with elimination, arthritis, rheumatism and migraine headaches. Boredom and confinement, for whatever reason, can actually bring on an emotional breakdown. They simply have to keep busy and active, both mentally and physically.

FRIENDS AND SOCIAL LIFE

The Gemini man enjoys many friends but few close friendships. This is because he tires of close association with the same people over a long period of time. At your parties he will positively scintillate and easily charm all your guests. He really enjoys parties because they provide a stage to display his wit and eloquence.

CLOTHES HE LIKES TO SEE YOU WEAR

He likes variety in your clothes, so you can wear almost anything you like but avoid wearing the same costume too often. He especially likes yellow and beige. Do your homework on your clothes and keep your wardrobe up-to-date so you can be ready to go at a moment's notice to whatever treat he has planned. He doesn't like to be kept waiting.

HOW TO ENTERTAIN YOUR GEMINI

First of all, plan a party and include other people. For the Gemini, parties are a stage where he can dazzle, make witty conversation and tell hilarious stories. He will keep things lively and entertain your other guests. He likes people and he is sure to respond to your invitation to drop over for cocktails and games. He is very good at charades, mental games and even old-fashioned scavenger hunts. They give him a chance to move about, use his active, agile mind to its best advantage and most important, impress others. He is something of a ham. Here is a sample menu for your cocktail do:

Fishhouse Punch
or Other Simple to Prepare Punch
(Not too Much Pow—You don't Want
Your Guests too Smashed to Play Games)
Dips   Pate
Crackers   Raw Vegetables

When you come back from your scavenger hunt you might want to serve spaghetti or chili with breadsticks and plenty of hot coffee. This should be an easy menu to put together and still leave you time to admire your most important guest.

For your second invitation, assuming he shows signs of properly appreciating lovely, desirable, sexy you, you might try a dinner tete a tete:

Green Salad
Baked Salmon with Bacon Strips
Brocoli/Lemon Slice   Baked Potatoes
Sherbet with Cookies

Serve tea instead of coffee, he's apt to prefer it. He will have enough nervous energy without zapping him up into the stratosphere with too much coffee. A liquer after dinner, such as creme de menthe or an Alexander, might provide the proper, soothing touch. Let him take it from there.

FOODS THAT GRATIFY HIM

Light simple meals appeal to your Gemini. Forget the heavy sauces and gravies. Serve him some lightly seasoned sea food. He will enjoy unusual dishes he has not tasted before. Serve him fruits and vegetables of all kinds. Good conversation at meal time stimulates his appetite. Too much coffee increases his nervous excitement and he isn't overly fond of alcohol. Dreamy music on your stereo will have a soothing effect on him during dinner.

WHAT KIND OF HUSBAND WILL HE BE?

As a husband he will be very proud of his home. He will look upon it as a safe and welcome refuge at the end of the day. He likes to come home to you to be soothed and rejuvenated. He will be content with you as long as you never bore him. In fact, that is the principal reason he chose to marry you in the first place.

Mornings will be interesting. You never know what kind of a mood he will wake up with. He may carry his worries over from the day before and have difficulty getting up. If his previous day was exciting and stimulating, he may still be keyed up the next morning. It all depends on what happened before.

He will make every effort to have a gracious home where he can entertain guests who are interesting and willing to engage in intellectual conversation.

He can be very moody and irritable with you at times. Don't overreact. The key is the light, loving touch. Don't try to domineer him, he will simply leave home. His moods change easily. You must show him affection and tell him how much you do appreciate what he does for you and the home. This will swing him back to normal.

Don't be too upset if he engages in a harmless flirtation. He is charming to women and will probably always enjoy their company because he does thrive on admiration. His flirtations, if any, will be meaningless to him. He has no intention of breaking up his home. He will be very supportive if you want to involve yourself in outside activities. While you pursue worthwhile accomplishments of your own but still find plenty of time for him, the two of you will be a truly happy couple.

WHAT KIND OF FATHER WILL HE BE?

Your children will be a powerful and stabilizing factor in your marriage. Your Gemini husband will be deeply attached to them and they will love him. As youngsters, he will sometimes relate to them as if he were another child and tell them wonderful stories. He will happily entertain them and their friends and delight in watching them grow. He will encourage them to finish college because he is a great believer in education. He may not always be available when you take them to the hospital for minor surgery but he will be a delightful companion during their convalescence. He will leave the matter of their discipline to you. He will want his children to be gay and joyous, free and unrestrained.

He will see to it that his children have financial security. He will allow them to make their own chioces as young adults and will not cling to them when they leave the home.

GEMINI CO-WORKERS

You probably have been able to spot the Gemini in your office by now, they are hard to miss. They seem to flit about on a different orbit than the rest of us mortals. Where Virgos can organize details, Aries can come up with unbelievably original ideas and Aquarians can think in wildly abstract terms, Geminis can easily do all three. While they hate to organize, they can, if the situation demands it, and they neatly relegate the details of the job to an underling. They don't have the staying power of the Virgo or the dedication of the Aquarian, but they are charming and ingenious and they can put on a one-man show that is dazzling.

As a salesman he is a genius. He can sell himself and his company.

Never mind that he may sell people things they will never use. He is equally good on the road meeting the customers or on the golf course or tennis court. His gift of gab operates fluently anywhere and he never stops selling. He is also a genius with an expense account and is not averse to padding it. All for the good of the firm, of course. One Gemini, who, when asked how he was doing, would reply, "everyone I can and the weak ones twice." Granted, he did have an affliction in his chart, but nevertheless he was not unusual, only more honest than most twins.

What about the females? The typist who is the fastest, the girl on the switchboard who is able to do some filing, answer questions and keep her phone lines in remarkable order, has to be a Gemini. They are whizzes at doing two or even three things at once. This girl won't disconnect the boss while he is talking to Tokyo. She can also charm the customers she meets at the front desk.

Both sexes are good at asking for raises and making their bosses think it was their idea to up the salary. They can make a raise seem perfectly logical and deserved. They usually shoot up the ladder faster than more pedantic signs such as Taurus and Capricorn. They also don't get along well with these two signs. If you want to see some fireworks, watch an Aries argue with a Gemini. However, in a sales office these two can be extremely valuable. They are the ones who come up with the fantastic ideas. Let the Virgos, Capricorns and Taureans iron out the details.

GEMINI BOSSES

The Gemini boss is probably in this position without really knowing why he got there. Once there he may be rather uncomfortable. This because he is so restless; it's even hard for him to sit still behind a desk for any length of time. (He never had that problem when he was out on the road selling for his company.) The ordinary run of the mill detail involved in leading a large company quickly becomes depressing to the Gemini. He is very unhappy if he is forced into a routine nine-to-five position. If he has a job as a trouble shooter or management consultant, management representative, or marketing analyst, some sort of position where he can move around, he is much happier. Most Geminis, when they achieve their upper echelon job, rapidly sort out the organizational details and turn them over to others. If he is a new boss and you were working for the company before he came, you will see a tremendous change as soon as he gains his promotion. Everything seems to go faster. He is on the phone constantly. Remember the stories of Kennedy calling up a surprised and sleepy Congressman at three in the morning to discuss something that just came into his head? He is impatient with time, and wants things done now, not tomorrow.

Just because the office staff have always done things "that way" will not impress him a bit. When he comes poking around to see how a particular job functions he is not going to be impressed with tradition. In fact, that could be the very reason he plans to change things; "things" being whatever was done before. On the other hand, unlike Taurus, he will not be dogmatic. His opinions are generally flexible.

Although his agile mind needs the give and take of human interaction, he will not become overly friendly with his employees. He needs people around as sounding boards, but not particularly as bosom friends. He sort of categorizes people according to their ideas and personalities. He will only notice an employee for a short time and then he is off on another tangent. It isn't that he doesn't respect his employees or their individuality, it's just that he views them rather impersonally. Office intrigues will have a difficult time flourishing in a Gemini run establishment. He can spot an intrigue a mile away, before it even gets a foothold.

Enjoy him while you can because he is apt to flit off to greener pastures on a moment's notice. You can learn a good deal about human nature from watching him cajole, wheedle, tell stories, sell himself and his ideas. He really is a one man show and like mercury, impossible to hold. Just when you think he has slowed down, he is darting off somewhere else.

CANCER

June 21-July 22

HIS ABILITY TO LOVE A WOMAN

Ruled by the moon, a cardinal sign, Cancer is the sign of the crab, and, like the crab, he goes steadily, relentlessly after what he wants. If you sense that he may be thinking about you as a wife, you are very likely right. He is really a homebody and he is dating girls for only one reason, to find a wife and not just any girl will do.

He is rather prudish and expects his prospective wife to have very high morals. However, he has strong sexual desires and he may sleep with a girl he feels does not qualify as a wife. He has little regard for a girl who sleeps around, even though she sleeps with him. This dichotomy requires adroit handling; one wrong move and he's gone.

Because Cancer is rather domestic, he may want to cook for you in his home. You can look forward to a delicious seafood dish and the perfect wine. In a rather old-fashioned way he is tender and down-to-earth, considerate of every female. If he takes you out to dinner, and he probably will, he will choose a small intimate restaurant with candlelight and soft music. He will avoid bright lights and loud music.

43

You may expect questions about your family background and where you went to school. This man is checking you out and evaluating your answers. If you ask him similar questions, he may retreat into his shell; he is basically a shy man. Wait until he is more relaxed and knows you better before you try to find out his vital statistics. If he has had an unhappy childhood he won't answer any of your questions about that, anyway. Home and family mean more to him than to any of the other signs and an unhappy home is shattering to a Cancer.

Cancer is a very conservative man and you probably won't believe some of his jokes. They date back to Abbott and Costello.

He loves art and music and may be quite talented and creative himself. Your dates may include visits to art galleries and concerts.

He is a very idealistic man and tends to put his women on a pedestal. Be careful you don't fall off and disenchant him. His wife and his family, when he achieves this longed for state, will be his entire world.

Unfortunately, there is an afflicted Cancer type, as there is in every sign, and this particular Cancer type can be very difficult. If you criticize him he will spend an hour explaining to you why you are wrong. He simply can't be criticized. There seems to be a basic insecurity which requires him to continually justify his actions. If you do fall in love with him you will need to remember that the only way to have peace is to continually praise him; you can't praise him too much. This man may have had a very damaging childhood or there may have been some illness early in his life which left an emotional scar, so he needs constant reassuring.

The garden variety Cancer you are hopefully dating will probably not have such tremendous needs for love and ego building. He will be a tender man. If you quarrel expect him to suffer deeply and retreat silently, unless he has an Aries or Gemini rising, that is. Then he will defend himself vigorously. If you do quarrel, he won't call you if he is really hurt. Call him. He needs your reassurance. If he is left alone he will be inclined to brood about you and he may come up with pretty surprising conclusions. Once he gets an idea in his head you may have difficulty getting him to change his mind. When you are getting along well you may think you really don't know him. This is because he is so reticent about his deepest feelings. Only another Cancer can really understand him. If you happen to be a Cancer yourself you are both endowed with extraordinary empathy and you will have a marriage made in heaven, one that will go on happily for years and years. If you are not a Cancer, be content to allow him to cherish and love you and as time goes by he will be able to reveal his deeper feelings to you.

RELATIVES

No other sign of the zodiac admires his relatives more than Cancer. He loves family picnics, family reunions, family birthday parties, family anniversaries. He expects to spend all holidays with his family. He will treat his parents and grandparents with great respect. The ethics and principles they taught him as a child will remain with him all his life. He will feel it his duty to help any of his family financially or any other way he can. He will want to meet your family and will make a very good impression because he will also treat them with the greatest respect. His mother's opinion is of the utmost importance to him and when he introduces you to her he will be delirious with joy at her approval of you as a mate.

MONEY AND CAREER

Cancer likes the finer things of life but he isn't too ambitious. He would like to have all the goodies but he wants them to drop into his lap without too much effort on his part. Ordinarily he is not too successful in partnerships because he is apt to be overly critical of his partner. If his feelings are hurt he is often unable to affect an open confrontation with his partner and straighten things out. He is more likely to retreat in silence. If he does find himself in a partnership he will tend to stay longer than most people, even if he is unhappy. He is most successful as a supervisor in a large firm and will understand his employees very well. Because he is so emphathetic he is adept at smoothing over difficult situations.

He does very well working with people on a one to one basis, such as direct selling or service. He becomes discouraged rather easily and sometimes does not have the stamina to keep going when he is temporarily defeated. If he does achieve some success, he gains confidence and can go onto more and more successes.

As a doctor he is very successful and his patients trust him. He is able to gain their confidence and they are able to discuss their most sensitive emotional problems with him because they know he understands. Cancers make very popular teachers. They like children and again are able to understand them well. The crab is capable of great loyalty to whatever work he is doing and when he wants to, can be very tenacious.

Many Cancers accumulate a comfortable supply of the world's goods by the time they are ready to retire. Some of their money is tied up in stocks, bonds, real estate and annuities. Your Cancer man will carefully investigate any investments he plans to make, and once he has committed himself will hold onto it. He is not much given to speculation in the stock market. The crab is very careful about money and always seems to be able to save some even on a very limited income. He will do well as a financial consultant handling other people's money. He has a very analytical mind and understands monetary matters.

He may not talk about it, but he usually has a rather neatly itemized budget, even if he doesn't account for every penny. He can be quite thrifty with himself, although he will not hesitate to spend money on gifts for loved ones. He is apt to be so quiet about his financial affairs you probably will not be aware of what his financial goals are.

HEALTH AND DIET

Your Cancer man has a rather delicate constitution. If he works too hard and becomes upset he may suffer from indigestion. If he really is under great emotional stress his stomach will rebel and he will be unable to eat. Coffee and tea sometimes upset him and he does not drink much liquor. He may have a small glass of champagne to celebrate a family party. He needs more rest than other signs. When he does become ill, he is apt to imagine that he is more seriously ill than he actually is. A wise woman will help to soothe his fears during convalescence so that he can relax and recover more rapidly. A crab's emotions have a great deal to do with his illnesses. Some crabs become so chronically tense and nervous they develop ulcers. The stomach seems to be the spot where illness strikes them. They need a woman who is tender and understanding, one who will fuss over them when they are ill.

FRIENDS AND SOCIAL LIFE

Because he senses their thoughts and feelings his friends adore him. He is loyal, faithful and true to all his friends. He remembers special events sometimes for years, much to the delight of his friends.

He may have trouble with some relationships because his feelings are so easily hurt. If he feels that a friend has been disloyal, unethical or cruel he is deeply wounded. He may not drop the friend but he will never feel quite the same about that person and he won't be able to demand an explanation. The friend may never know what he did to offend, but he will be aware that the friendship has cooled.

Your Cancer man likes to entertain at home. Because he is so ethical he will not use friends to further his business ambitions, he feels this would be disloyal to them. He keeps his friends for years, some for a lifetime.

CLOTHES HE LIKES TO SEE YOUR WEAR

Flower prints, ladylike pastels and lingerie heavily frosted with lace turn him on. If you have any antique pins or rings, wear them and mention that they belonged to your great grandmother. Dresses and blouses of greens, white and shimmery sea tones are good. He may surprise you with a fabulous saphire ring.

HOW TO ENTERTAIN A CANCER

Select a weekend or an evening when you know he doesn't have to get up early the next morning. How about a fondue party made with either meat or cheese and hunks of good French bread? Your love likes to cook and he can help you set up the fondue pot and cut the meat and bread. A little wine, a salad, and you two can have a nice, fun time spearing the meat or bread and dipping it in the fondue. You could mention the old custom that whoever loses their portion into the pot has to forfeit a kiss . . .

Fondue
Green Salad with Strips of Chicken, Cheese,
Tomato, Bean Srouts, Mushrooms and a
Good Oil and Vinegar Dressing
White or Rose Wine
Fruit and Cheese for Desert

Have everything ready to put together when he gets there. Save a few things for him to help you with. If you serve wine in a corked bottle have a fantastic cork remover so he doesn't have to wrestle with a bottle of wine that has pieces of the cork floating around—this won't improve your efficiency rating. If it is cool and you have a fireplace, lay a fire for him to light. If it is too warm for a fire you could plan a beach or a mountain picnic.

Homemade Coleslaw
with Cucumbers and Your Favorite Dressing
Fried Chicken
Homemade Bread or Rolls with Plenty of Butter and Honey
Egg in Dill Sauce
Wine Served in Wine Glasses—Add Pizzazz!

Bring your china plates and silver and a pretty old-fashioned checkered tablecloth. Pack all this in a big picnic basket. If you hang around much with your Cancer you will go on lots of picnics, maybe even boat picnics. Take along a blanket and some pillows for you to languish upon while he tells you what a great cook you are. When you get home you might surprise him with some homemade vanilla ice cream you have prepared already, packed in ice to mellow. Add some chewy chocolate cookies and you will really impress him. How many girls know how to do so many things so well and look and smell so delicious too!

FOODS THAT GRATIFY HIM

Cancers like seafoods, green salads, toast, hot chocolate, chocolate dishes of all kinds and wine and beer. Some prefer Scotch. Sometimes a nice juicy steak and carefully seasoned green salad with oil and vinegar dressing will please him. Make sure you have soft light and of course, the music he likes on the stereo when he comes to your home for dinner. Plan a quiet, unhurried meal, seasoned with tender, loving conversation. Loud noises and arguments can upset him so that he won't be able to enjoy his dinner and, incidentally, and most importantly, you. He will appreciate your efforts to please him and will tell you so. He knows how much compliments mean to a cook and hostess.

WHAT KIND OF HUSBAND WILL HE BE?

When a crab marries he has achieved his goal. This is really more important to him than business success. Once he is married he is married for keeps. He is possessive, jealous and perhaps a bit dictatorial because his wife and home mean so much to him. He is very unlikely to stray from you but if he does, briefly, he is careful to keep it away from his beloved home. If you are a sensible wife you will forgive and forget. The crab is worth it. He may come back wanting you to punish him to banish his guilt feelings.

Keeping his home in good repair will be a labor of love. He will contentedly repair your washer, your stopped-up sink or rewire your favorite antique lamp. Tell him how clever he is and how much you appreciate him.

A Cancer can be moody, often for no apparent reason. It may be that he is overly tired and just needs a good night's sleep, or possibly just a nap. See to it that he has sufficient rest and a tranquil home. You will need to discipline yourself so that you do not become irritated by his moods; they are a part of his nature, and just like the tides they will return again and again.

On weekends when he doesn't have to go to work he will not rise with the dawn. He does enjoy extra sleep, so see that he gets it. Cancers love cuddling and physical demonstrations of love. Plan ahead for plenty of time to love him when he is home. Bring him breakfast in bed once in a while. He really deserves it. After all, he is a pretty remarkable fellow, he married you, didn't he? You will be a very special love to him forever and ever and ever.

WHAT KIND OF FATHER WILL HE BE?

Your Cancer husband will love his children deeply but he maybe rather critical of their upbringing. He has some pretty well conceived ideas of how children should behave and he will try to get them to conform to his value standards. If his children are strong-willed, he will have difficulty understanding them. If they hurt his feelings he may crawl into his shell leaving you to deal with the situation. Generally, a Cancer father is warm and loving to his children. There are exceptions to this rule. One Cancer who loves his three children deeply was continually wiping their chins in restaurants, making sure their elbows weren't on the table and constantly picking at them when they were small. Surprisingly the kids accepted this and told each other that's "just how Pop is." Apparently the kids knew he loved them and could overlook his fussiness. Most Cancers aren't that picky-picky. They will gladly help you with the care of the children and will see that they have every advantage possible. Make sure that you do not lavish so much love on the children that you neglect their father. Of all the signs, he will be the most deeply hurt by your neglect.

CANCER CO-WORKERS

Cancer is a cardinal sign and cardinal signs are born to lead, not follow. The Crab takes orders gracefully but he is only serving so willingly because he is following his own program. He wants power and influence. He doesn't want power like Capricorn for the status it brings; or power like Scorpio because he likes to bend others to his will; the crab wants power because power spells security.

Cancer drags his little shell around with him and clambers steadily toward his goal. The denizens of the deep may scare him silly sometimes, but he tries hard not to show it, and he keeps on going. If he is hurt too badly he will crawl back in his shell and have another go at it after he's gotten himself sorted out. Female crabs act pretty much the same in an office. Sometimes they drag their shells around sideways, back and forth but they usually get where they are headed.

Cancers also need appreciation. A pat on the back won't make up for a raise, but it may keep the crab around a bit longer while he checks out the office to see what the possibilities are. For one thing, Cancer finds it acutely painful to pull up stakes and go out in the cruel world looking for another job. The crab would prefer to stay where he is and head for the top there if possible. Job hunting is very scary for crabs. All those interviews with strangers.

There is a charming, delightful, magical quality to the Cancer child. She hoards old popsickle sticks, old school papers, out of date newspapers, outgrown clothes, dolls and toys. She never throws anything away. Adult Cancers feel the same way about their jobs.

Relatives are important to Cancers. Cancers sometimes need time off to cope with family problems. If there is a crab employee going through a divorce or separation, the office will be awash in tears and gloom. Tears and grief notwithstanding, she will not allow herself or her children to be cheated out of child support. There is no more protective mother in all the zodiac when it comes to taking care of her little crabs, unless Leo's cubs are threatened. Either parent will fight for their little one's best interests. Cancer may have a bit of an edge over Leo in this respect. Cancer can be a bit more businesslike than Leo. Leo gets fogged up with the sort of details that Cancer sees through clearly.

Cancers go to lunch with their mothers a lot. If you have something to talk over with a Cancer, take them to lunch. Crabs come alive in restaurants. Their eyes light up, they sparkle and bubble. Being around all that food puts them at ease. All is right with their world. Of course, not having to pick up the check does help. Dining across the table from a happy, witty Cancer is a treat not to be missed. They will keep you entertained from soup to desert. Cancers are marvelous story tellers and have a funny, happy wit.

A wounded crab in the office can be a pretty depressing sight. They pout in silence, their unhappiness is a physical aura. They are not above resorting to cleverness or deceit to get what they want. Sometimes the victim doesn't know his job was in danger until it's gone. The Cancer has grabbed it up—it was a bigger and better shell. They are faithful employees if treated with understanding.

CANCER BOSSES

Ninety-eight per cent of the time, your Cancer boss is all business. He is there to make money which will provide for his love, his wife, his children, his trips, and most of all, his old age. Business is pretty serious to Cancers. There won't be any funny stuff going on in that office. He might grin a bit at a goof from an overconfident competitor. That is funny. You are funny too if you ask for a raise before you have convinced him you know what you are doing. Most of the time your office will be humorless and a bit grim, but efficient.

You may discover he has some food and drink squirreled away in his office. It isn't that he gets so hungry, its just that it is comforting to him to know there are snacks to soothe his jumpy tummy. Food is a security blanket. Cancer rules the stomach and the emotions.

He may have some good prints hanging on the office walls, perhaps his family coat of arms and he certainly will have any diplomas or certificates he has won, proudly displayed. Of course, he will have his wife and children's photos in pretty frames. The crab thinks of his office as an extension of his home. When it comes to decorations, his application of style, design and texture come together in a pleasant, flowing manner. Many Cancers love to grow plants and have a natural aptitude for making them flourish. If your boss is female her office may look like a jungle.

He will never forget a mistake, a cut, or a kindness. In men, he expects the trousers to be creased and women employees must wear conservative office-type clothes.

A curious trait of Cancer is his ability to horse trade. He can figure out what people need and then sell it to them. That Cancerian empathy, again. He was trading marbles when he was six and had a paper route at twelve. This is true even if his family was affluent. Thrift and the desire for money are born in him.

Cancers, both male and female, live in shells. When they are hurt, or the world suddenly becomes too threatening, they crawl back in. If your Cancer boss suddenly gets very moody and sits for awhile looking out the window, don't be surprised. The crab has been wounded or frightened, or maybe its just because the moon is full. The full moon has tremendous effects on Cancers, you never know how they are going to react. They may get very moody and irritable. Cancers are deeply sensitive, even when the moon isn't full. They hurt a lot more than they ever show.

There is an afflicted type of Cancer boss, hopefully you don't work for one. She might spell the girl at the switchboard so she can listen in on conversations. She has office favorites and office not so favorites. Fortunately, Cancer bosses like this are rare, but they do exist.

Cancer women bosses are not rare however, because Cancer women are just as strongly motivated to find security as male Cancers. Cancer women usually don't like housework as much as they like offices. This seems to be true even if they are married. They love their homes, but they enjoy sharpening their wits in the business world. In order to keep the homestead shining, they hire domestic help. For all their tender hearts, Cancers are tough-minded in the business world, male or female.

Remember the Cancer memory. He or she has computerized the data on you; when you arrive, when you leave, mistakes you have made, over-time you have put in and good things you have done for the company beyond your job duties. Cancer remembers everything good and bad. Do your job, don't take advantage and you will have job security.

leo
July 23-August 22

HIS ABILITY TO LOVE A WOMAN

Love is more important to a Leo than any other sign. Your Leo man may be very successful but he must have love to be truly happy. When he finds true love he is buoyant, courageous, magnanimous and creative. Leo the Lion knows he is the king of the world and he loves you to tell him so. He rejoices in sex and is a lusty, earthy lover who sometimes delights in the ribald. Because he tends to be so dramatic, you may think he is being a showoff. He is just being his own exuberant self. He is fiery, demanding, tenderly affectionate and passionate.

He expects you to be the follower. If you fail to be such, he may become angry and leave you in a rage, or worse yet, coldly turn away from you. You will not get him back.

The sign of Leo represents the ego. He needs praise more than food, his ego is the center of his life. It is also the sign of diplomacy. However, he can become rather tyranical if he finds that diplomacy isn't getting him wnat he wants. Usually he is such a genial, popular fellow that he is successful by the sheer force of his personality. Sometimes he can be so charming he gets what he wants without even trying.

He trusts people and is much more honest than your friends of other signs. He tends to believe the best of everyone. If he is interested in you he will be very loyal. Don't be unfaithful or dishonest with this man, you will break his great heart and though he may forgive you he won't forget. He will never stoop to petty, underhanded deals and he detests viscious gossip.

Your Leo man will want to build on his own castle in his own little world, with him as the king and you as his royal consort. He is very proud and simply cannot conceive that you might do anything to bring disgrace upon him. Even if you should, he will stick by you through thick and thin.

As you may expect, he will make the decisions as to where you will go for dinner and entertainment. This is as natural as breathing to him. He will take you to the very best restaurants he can afford and enjoy ordering for you. He will bask in your praise because he knows that he deserves it. He has a tendency to be quite moody, but just stay out of his way until his mood passes. He probably won't tell you he is sorry but he will buy you something lavish. In fact, you can expect to be gifted with all sorts of expensive, carefully chosen presents for no reason at all except that he likes you and wants to make you happy.

Leos are easy to identify. First of all, you will usually see them around town at all the "in" spots. He will be the one with the stately bearing, a dignified air, and he is probably the center of attention. His hair will be distinctive for one reason or another. Sometimes it resembles a lion's mane, thick and sweeping back from a high, broad forehead. His walk will be rather lazy and slow, but very graceful. He does not plod along like a Taurean or barely touch the ground as a Gemini.

There are blue eyed Leos but many of them will have brown eyes, that at first are soft and melting but can crackle and snap with fire. Hair color could be dark or redish blonde and often wavy.

Leo is terribly proud but also terribly vulnerable. He thrives on compliments and is crushed if he feels he isn't being appreciated. If this occurs, he may retreat quietly, or he may pull out all the stops and use his dramatic ability and rant and rave. His roar, however, is worse than his bite, and most people know it, even children. A peculiarity of this sign is the natural affinity Leos have for children. They seem to have vibes that draw children to them. Unfortunately they often experience sorrow through children, but more about that later in another section.

Leos love responsibility. They carry it lightly and thrive under loads that would make other signs stagger and fall. Leo may roar and complain about the responsibility he has, but just try to lighten his load and you will see that he really doesn't want any help. A peculiar quirk of the personality is his high pain threshold. Proud as he is he will never admit it, but a visit to the dentist can terrify him. Leo secretly feels he is not as strong or courageous as others. Remember the Lion in the Wizard of Oz who was searching for the gift of true courage? This is where you come in, you simply cannot praise him too much, but make sure it is genuine praise. You don't want to ever try to fool him—he will never trust you again, and his great heart will be broken.

RELATIVES

Leo is very fond of his relatives and has a strong sense of family ties. He may travel long distances to attend reunions and he expects to spend Christmas and other holidays with his family. He is very loyal to his relatives but then he is loyal with everyone he likes. He loves to be the center of interest in the family circle.

MONEY AND CAREER

Your Leo man will probably be an executive, for he is a natural born leader. He is adept at inspiring others but not so good at handling details. Responsibility brings out his very best qualities and as the head of any organization he is tops. He will be successful in any of the professions for he just naturally puts his best foot forward. He could be a very able trial lawyer but not a very happy estate lawyer. Details and routine bore him. His flair for the dramatic will make him a well liked teacher. Leos like children and children seem to respond especially well to Leos.

As a salesman he will excel as he will sell himself first and then have no difficulty selling his product. The stage and dramatic arts are natural mediums for him. Many movie and stage personalities are Leos, or have Leo rising.

He will be much happier working for himself than for an organization unless he has freedom to use his own creative abilities. Partnerships will be difficult for him because he will probably be so honest that he will find it impossible to believe he could be cheated.

Manual work will not interest him and deep down he will feel that it really is beneath him. He is not very skilled at working with his hands and isn't too well coordinated.

Your Leo man will need an important job or a lofty ambition to sustain him or he will feel depressed and lonely. He will have great tenacity in following through with his plans in whatever line of work he chooses and will enjoy discussing them with you. Be sure to let him know how much you admire him, particularly when he is momentarily unsuccessful. You probably won't be called upon to cheer him up too often. However, if he really gets down in the dumps he is a sorry sight indeed.

HEALTH AND DIET

A Leo man is so bursting with health and vigor it is hard to imagine him any other way. Even when he is ill you think he is dramatizing again because he will look so healthy. He loves to eat and will cram all sorts of rich food into his long suffering stomach. The fact is, a Leo has such a strong constitution he is rarely ill and he has the ability to recover quickly. As you might expect his illnesses are sudden and dramatic, like everything else about him. He often runs high fevers, is prone to sudden accidents, but immune to chronic, lingering illnesses. Whatever illness overtakes him will be unprogrammed. He will feel great one minute and the next minute might suddenly turn his ankle, breaking a bone in his foot. They suffer from problems with the feet, legs or ankles, problems with the reproductive organs, and have either very strong hearts or weak hearts. They never do anything half way. They are either in fantastic good health or dying. If your Leo comes down with some ailment he probably will dramatize it but when he realizes this puts him at a disadvantage, he is sick and you are well and strong, he will recover rapidly. Staying in bed is fun and flattering at first, and Leo can be very lazy, but it usually doesn't last very long. When they work they work, when they play they play.

Usually your Leo will have bounding good health and almost limitless energy.

FRIENDS AND SOCIAL LIFE

He will have lots of friends from every walk of life. He is not snobbish and couldn't be if he tried. He will, however, discard friends who do not live up to his high ideals of fair play and integrity. He likes parties but he doesn't like senseless small talk and is bored with large, impersonal cocktail parties. He will like to entertain you and his friends in his own home and will spare no expense to see that his guests have a good time.

CLOTHES HE LIKES TO SEE YOU WEAR

He will like to see you in vivid corals, bright reds, yellows and expensive gold jewelry. Don't wear costume jewelry, he doesn't like imitation anything. Dress for him, he will love you for it. Whatever you wear, make sure it looks expensive, even if it isn't.

FOODS THAT GRATIFY HIM

Feed him anything that is rich and delicious. He loves good food of all kinds as long as it is tastefully seasoned and sauced. French pastries, buttery sauces, exotic out-of-season foods or even foods he never heard of, he will enjoy them all. No cheap casserole dishes for this man, he won't criticize you but he won't love you for it either. Your apartment should be spanking clean, soft music, rosy lights and plenty of soft, plushy cushions. This man likes his comfort in a rich setting.

WHAT KIND OF HUSBAND WILL HE BE?

A Leo husband adopts a protective role and may be rather dominating at times. He will expect you to run a beautifully ordered home in which he can entertain lavishly. He will not scrimp on your clothing allowance and will expect to see you well dressed in the very best that he can afford. He will provide all the luxuries he can and will look forward to bringing home the fruits of his labors. In fact, if he couldn't lay the spoils of his efforts at your feet he wouldn't feel that the struggle was worth it. If you don't show him that you appreciate him he will be deeply hurt.

A Leo values his privacy highly, perhaps more than any other sign. Your home, even though it may be in the city, should give him a feeling of isolation.

If he finds that he has married an unsuitable wife he will stick with his marriage simply because he has agreed to do so. He may flirt, even in a happy marriage, but his flirtations are rather harmless. He will not indulge in petty squabbles with you.

Whatever you do, remember this one tip when dealing with your Leo love—don't ever try to make him jealous. It just won't work. He is JEALOUS. He knows you are enchanting and lovely or he wouldn't have picked you in the first place. Dalliance on street corners and bars will turn him off immediately and bruise his tender ego. He could deck someone he feels is overly friendly if he is pushed too far. Of course, the same rule does not apply to him. He appreciates beauty and that includes beautiful women. But don't confuse this fondness for pretty women with having affairs, he will be a loyal and a faithful husband as long as he knows you are a loyal and a faithful wife. In his mind, a girlfriend is not too different from a wife. Be sure to play it straight with him until you have determined how you really feel; if this is the man you want to spend the rest of your life with, show it. If you do arouse his jealousy he will just retreat to another girl who is more appreciative. All Leos live for love, and they are either engaged, married, in the middle of a torrid love affair or miserably unhappy because of a romantic breakup. Don't let your Leo go running around loose because you unwisely played games with him. There are other predators on the prowl who find a Leo is just what they want in their lives.

If you marry him you may be awakened at the crack of dawn with a very angry husband on your hands. He will be impatient to be about the business of the day and feeling exuberant. Only when he has been on the go for weeks at a time will he sleep late.

This husband will be neat and fastidious about his personal habits. He will take great pains with his appearance.

WHAT KIND OF FATHER WILL HE BE?

Of all signs of the zodiac, he will be the most devoted father. He loves children and they love him. He will make great sacrifices of his time and money for his children. He feels deeply his obligations to his children. At times he may be rather dictatorial and can lose his temper easily but this soon blows over. He doesn't sulk or brood and never holds a grudge. He will teach his children honesty and generosity by his own example. He will go with you to his children's recitals and school plays. He may even be a leader in the Little League if he doesn't have to handle too many details. He will want to see his daughters well dressed and won't begrudge the expense for their finery. If his children don't turn out well he will be deeply hurt, especially if they disgrace his name. If you already have children of your own when you marry him he will open his heart to them. They will become his children and he will have the same high expectations for them as for his own.

It is a tragedy that many Leos, for all their love of children, often have small families. They may suffer great sorrow because of their children. The generous, hard-working Leo may suddenly wake up and find that his chick and child have flown the nest, never to return, even for brief visits. Or he may lose his child through death. Many Leo men lose their children through divorce, despite their tender efforts to keep in touch and be a father, even at long distance. Needless to say, this hurts Leo greatly, although he probably won't speak of it very freely.

LEO CO-WORKERS

You won't see too many Leo co-workers, male gender at least. They are headed toward executive jobs where they can use their leadership abilities. If your office is one where there are possibilities of advancement he will probably stay. Details are hateful to most Leos, and a dull hum-drum job will quickly send him looking for a more dramatic one. Speaking of drama, you will find many Leos in the entertainment field. Arlene Dahl, Lucille Ball, Mike Douglas, Alfred Hitchcock are Leos, to name a few.

If they aren't bogged down with endless details, young Leos are perfect in sales and promotional jobs. They are natural actors and actresses and are great at entertaining customers and making a good impression for the company. Later, as they mature, astute management would be smart to keep moving them up. Leos are so responsible and hardworking that they easily assume managerial roles. One of the reasons why they like authority is because they love to tell people how to solve their problems. They are surprisingly good at sorting out the problems in their own lives. If the Leo in your office doesn't have enough authority you may find them telling the messenger girl how to shorten her run and make it more efficient, the typist about a new ink eradicator, or how an amateur can grow orchids. They really love to teach and they are very good at it. They simply do not fit into dull drab office routine, and dull drab offices have a predictable effect upon them. They soon lose their sparkle and are apt to wither and fade, that is, if they last that long.

Female Leos keep the place lively. They decorate their offices in bright colors, orange and yellow are favorites, and both sexes love to have their name on a plaque on the desk, or better yet, on their very own office door. This is more important to Leo than the extra green in his pay check.

Female Leos love to flirt. They wear loose fitting, fluid clothing that seems to move with them. Male eyes readily turn as the dramatic sleek Lioness goes gliding through the office. Her clothes will be expensive and well cut. She would rather have two or three beautifully engineered outfits than several cheap bargain basement acquisitions.

Female Leos are hard workers and they are not clock watchers. There is nothing sneaky or devious about them, they are insulted if they feel they are not trusted to do their work. They do not indulge in gossip although they do like to know what is going on in the office. Bosses who are perceptive to the talent and loyalty they have on the payroll give their Leos recognition and compliments, this is meat and drink to them. Bosses who are petty or greedy will lose the Leo to another employer, one who is smart enough to see what an outstanding employee a Leo can be. Leos don't hang around forever waiting to be appreciated. They are very proud, and if they feel their role is too limiting or their talents wasted, off they go, out into the jungle that provides the challenge.

LEO BOSSES

Leos are born to lead. A Leo boss is happy at being a boss, it is what he aimed for long ago. He can teach, delegate authority and order others about the office to his heart's content. However, because of his dignity and pride he will not be as overbearing and dictatorial as this sounds. He will remember what it was like to be an employee, most of the time that is. He will truly luxuriate in passing off those hateful details to his secretary. Typical is the Leo boss who worked for a large aerospace company. He would toss letters on his secretary's desk shortly before noon and say, "Tell so and so 'maybe,' you know how to say it. No hurry, as long as I have it before I leave tonight." Then he would go off to a Chamber of Commerce meeting, thoroughly charm everyone and drop back in the office at 4:40 p.m. His secretary, a Virgo, would have the letters neatly typed for him. Sometimes he would compliment her, other times he would simply accept her work as his due. He is not above taking the credit for some of her clever phrasing.

The secretary was not resentful, she thought him an angel. He sent her mother flowers when she was in the hospital; lectured her boyfriend when he didn't help her move to her new apartment, an apartment he had found for her, incidentally cheaper and more attractive than her old one; redid her office with oranges and yellows and plush carpeting, and arranged for hand lotion and scented soap in the ladies room. If she had ever been short of money (being a Virgo, this was unlikely), he would have gladly lent her any amount to tide her over. Leos will lend money to almost anyone they think really needs it. Oddly enough, they are seldom repaid.

Leo Bosses are a storehouse of pep and energy. They are apt to hire youthful employees who are also full of pep and energy. They like to work, but they will make it fun, too. They are young at heart and enjoy being with young people. If you like your Leo boss, and of course you do, don't forget his birthday, he will be hurt. Invite the office staff and make a big fuss. He will want to know about your birthdays too, and about the names and ages of your children, your brothers and sisters and anyone important to you. This interest is sincere, he really cares.

If you have a money-saving idea that will make the office more efficient don't be afraid to suggest it. He is more likely to reward and compliment you than criticize you.

Your single Leo boss may be a bit amorous, after all, he does like beautiful women. Decide early on if you want to get involved or if you had better look for another job. This man is very affectionate and you don't want to injure his vanity and create problems for yourself in the office. If he is married you need have no fear, he is a faithful husband, even if he likes to flirt a bit and admire the scenery.

August 23 - September 22

VIRGO

August 23-September 22

HIS ABILITY TO LOVE A WOMAN

Virgo is the sign of the Virgin. As a man, he is not a very romantic lover although he may care for you deeply. For one thing, he is pretty involved in the details of daily living and he is very precise about his habits. He likes his clothes hung up in the closet with all the hooks facing one way, that kind of thing. His bedtime routine is concerned with his vitamin pills, his slippers and robe lined up by the bed and he will busy himself with his plans for the next day. In fact, he may just forget about sex altogether unless you are there handy to remind him. He actually isn't as interested in sex as the other signs of the zodiac and has more self control than any other sign.

He is completely surprised at a direct approach. He himself is not a very direct man and is pleasantly taken aback at a bold advance. When you once get him aroused he is curious about the details of your response. Later he will want to fuss over you and make you happy. He may bring you a cup of hot chocolate just as you are dropping off to sleep because it is good for you. He will not make love to you when you have the sniffles, but he will bring you cold remedies and Kleenex.

He is a very curious individual and he jumps to conclusions on the slightest pretext.

Once you capture his interest he may take to managing the details of your life because he wants to help you cope. You really don't have to scheme too much to hold him, he will hold you. At times he may seem obsessed with his health, his work, his vitamins and the accomplishments of tasks he has set for himself. Deep down in his heart he wants to be loved, for to him love means security. If he criticizes you, and he probably will, don't rebuff him or he will feel very sorry for himself. How *could* you criticize him? This may result in his falling in a morass of self pity because he feels he does not measure up. He is a perfectionist and needs a lot of praise, not criticism. He will repay you by being a tender and solicitous lover.

Don't let his naturally fuss-budgety notions put you off, he simply likes the details of his life well organized. He will be very loyal to you and he will sometimes surprise you with nice little gifts that are generally on the practical side. Although they may not be too romantic, his gifts will be chosen very carefully. This does not mean he is totally lacking in the romance department, its just that he is such a practical fellow. If you date a Virgo you can be sure he will have sufficient cash to pay the dinner check and he will go to great pains to see that you enjoy your evening with him. When he takes you out you may notice that he makes remarks about the unexceptional service in the restaurant or the cost of the drinks. He may not order food for himself but will insist that you order. Don't let this bother you, he has probably calculated his calorie intake and decided he shouldn't eat anything more that day.

A Virgo man likes to ask questions about you, and very personal questions at that. He may appear to be broadminded but he can be very stuffy if you read between the lines. Sometimes it is hard for him to be affectionate and spontaneous. Some Virgos are insensitive to the emotional needs of women.

He is a joiner and belongs to countless clubs and civic organizations. He will introduce you to the leaders of the community.

Virgos are worry-warts, but despite this unfortunate propensity there is a tranquility and serenity on Virgo features. Virgo eyes are clear and sparkling. Most are extremely attractive and they know it. You often see mirrors hung on the walls in Virgo offices. They like to check their appearance frequently.

A Virgo might keep an electric razor in his desk drawer and always shave about four in the afternoon. Even if he has hardly any beard and a skin as fine as a baby, he wants to be presentable at all times.

Virgos smile a great deal but they always seem to be hiding a secret worry. Most of the time Virgos are nice to be around. They do sometimes get cranky and nervous when they are around vulgar people. They really don't know how to cope with crudeness. They seem to dream a lot but they are about the most practical sign of the zodiac. If your particular Virgo doesn't seem down to earth he probably has his sign diluted by Pisces or Gemini.

He may have a bird or a cat as a pet. Virgos like small creatures. They help to stave off the always constant spectre of loneliness. He needs you tremendously because his world is so lonely. He needs your love to make it warm and cozy.

Virgos seem prone to enjoy success and good fortune and they may suddenly suffer misfortunes. He needs you to cheer him up.

RELATIVES

He will be dutiful to his relatives and may even sacrifice to care for an aged parent or to send a brother or sister to college. He will respond to their financial needs but otherwise will tend to take them for granted. He isn't much for family reunions and is apt to make an excuse to avoid partaking in the festivities.

MONEY AND CAREER

Virgo enjoys working with details. His memory is fantastic. He can be an outstanding bookkeeper, mathematician, research worker, statistician, librarian or art critic. He likes music and beauty. He is always very conscious of color. He probably will not be an executive because he gets so involved in details that he misses the big pictures. Also, he tends to give orders in an offensive manner. To him, an order is an order and he fails to see that he could gain more cooperation from his employees if he were more diplomatic.

He may be a very successful physican or an expert dietician. His ruling planet, Mercury, also rules hygiene and chemistry. Mercury stimulates his interest in literature, writing, speaking and teaching. What he lacks in imagination he makes up for in his ability to speak effectively. When he chooses he can be very charming and persuasive. He may have trouble adjusting himself to changes of jobs if this is forced upon him in times of a business slump, for example. He will look ahead and have another job lined up in the event he becomes unemployed. He receives good recommendations from employers. Virgo is the sign of quality.

If he operates his own business he will do well as long as he has a partner who can help him organize the overall business. Here again he gets so involved with fascinating but unimportant details that he neglects more important business decisions. He is the exact opposite of the Capricorn who can readily envision his business as a complete entity. Virgo can envision details as finished products and he has great mental agility. He is great at working out systems and methods of cataloging merchandise. He has the knack of placing the essential in the right spot for instant reference. Because he demands perfection in his own work and that of others he often rubs people the wrong way by his critical remarks. He is fearful of making mistakes and this holds him back from developing those really good ideas he has. If he can bring himself to present his ideas they emerge as finely polished jewels, perfect in every detail If he can let himself go and take a chance, he can go far.

HEALTH AND DIET

Health fascinates him. He may be a health nut. Not just one health program will do, he will keep experimenting until he finds one that is just right for him. He may have a somewhat technical knowledge of nutrition because he has read a great deal on the subject. He knows that good health is necessary in order for him to pursue his ambitions in life. If he becomes ill he can be very demanding about his medicines and his creature comforts. However, due to his vigilance, he is usually healthy. Virgos never over indulge in alcohol and food.

FRIENDS AND SOCIAL LIFE

Your Virgo man will choose his friends very carefully and they will be rather serious people. Once he has chosen them, they will stay his friends for a long time, unless he offends or hurts them with his criticism.

CLOTHES HE LIKES TO SEE YOU WEAR

Crisp fabrics that rustle, blues and grays conservatively styled clothes meet with his favor. He likes spanking clean hair, tied back with a ribbon. Everything about you should be immaculate, from your white underthings to your neatly shod feet. If there is a thread hanging from your hem he will let you know because he wants to be helpful. This man notices everything.

HOW TO ENTERTAIN VIRGO

Unless your special Virgo man has a Leo, Aries or Gemini rising sign he isn't going to be a very comfortable guest at one of your big cocktail parties. He would prefer a small dinner where you serve health foods. He would also enjoy a wilderness outing if he could be sure the drinking water was safe and he could find a washroom with hot and cold water.

If you decide to entertain him with a dinner or brunch, or even a picnic in the fresh pure air, keep the food simple and wholesome. Such a menu might be:

Broiled Chicken
Homemade Bread with Unbleached Flour
Steamed Brocoli with Lemon
Cheese, Fruit and White Wine for Desert

If he is a purist, substitute fruit juice for the wine. Any foods you cook for him should never be boiled or fried. Steam, bake or broil instead. Make all your bakery goods from whole grains from the health food store. Save the cooking water from the vegetables you steam to make gravies or sauces. Avoid starchy foods such as pasta, macaroni or noodles unless you can find them in the health food store. Use brown rice and don't rinse it. Your Virgo knows all about proper nutrition and he will be tickled pink to think you are willing to learn, and better yet to let him teach you. Even if you break up because he is so fussy you have learned a lot about how to live longer.

FOODS THAT GRATIFY HIM

Picnics are fun for Virgos. Serve him cold chicken, white wine and fresh fruit on a blue and white checkered tablecloth. He does not like heavy, exotic foods. He does like raw vegetables and fresh fruit in season. A really good cheese or an interesting trail mix will earn his approval. Coffee is about his only bad habit.

WHAT KIND OF HUSBAND WILL HE BE?

The Virgo man thinks marriage is the most practical and sensible arrangement for everyone. He expects to be married. As a husband he is quite reserved and it is difficult for him to show his feelings. He can, as you may suspect, become a very critical and fussy husband. He will provide you with a comfortable home and expect you to maintain it in apple pie order at all times. He will safeguard his home, but he will not have a very deep sentimental attitude toward it. A note of gaiety will crop up at unexpected times in your life together and at times he can be a tease.

He is not apt to stray unless you do and then he will explain that it was your fault. He believes in an eye for an eye and a tooth for a tooth.

He will not like deep philosophical discussions with you or your friends. He will like gaiety and witty people.

He is not apt to leap out of bed at the crack of dawn unless he has some unfinished work to do. When he has been out late the night before he will enjoy luxuriating in sleep.

Your Virgo man will prefer the quiet life although he may like to take long trips on his vacation, with you of course.

When he is on the brink of asking you to marry him he will cover his emotion with casual chatter. His actual proposal will be touchingly tender. He has looked for you for a long time. Once you are married he will love you deeply, tenderly on into the sunset years.

He will show great strength in dealing with financial emergencies. Hardships only increase his determination. He believes in an old fashioned marriage and will not like you to work. Providing for you is his pride and joy. He easily assumes the role of husband.

He will not be jealous but he does have a tendency to be possessive. Don't try to make him jealous just to get a rise out of him. If you persist he may become sufficiently outraged to walk away and never return. He will regard a clean, antiseptic break as the only solution for such behavior and that will be the end of your marriage. He doesn't believe in picking up the pieces of a beautiful antique vase or of a broken marriage. Both are spoiled and he likes to live with perfection. He is not perfect himself, but he does remember anniversaries, balances the checkbook, is gentle and considerate, soothes away your fears and waits on you when you are ill or out of sorts. He will be a faithful husband, given a chance, and love you devotedly.

WHAT KIND OF FATHER WILL HE BE?

As a father he will see that your children will have the best diet and medical care available. He probably will not be a sentimental or over-indulgent father, he will expect the children to do their share of the household chores. He is a doer and will instill this trait in his children. His tendency to criticize will be less with his children for he will love them dearly, but criticize he will. Help him to accept him as he is and to love and understand him. You simply can't change him. Probably he would be perfectly happy if he had no children at all. Be thankful he will try to be a good father when his children do arrive. If you marry a divorced Virgo father, be prepared for him to visit his children frequently. He does not take fatherhood lightly.

He will have good foresight and will see that his children have the advantage of the best education he can give them. He will enjoy stimulating their interests in art and beauty.

VIRGO CO-WORKERS

The shortcomings of the Virgo boss are what makes them such valued employees. They dote on bringing order out of chaos. Details are lovingly sorted. Everything is neatly catalogued. Perfection is sacred to this sign. Virgo makes an excellent proofreader, secretary, bookkeeper or most any ticklish, behind-the-scenes detail job. They have tremendous energy. They never do a job halfway. Perhaps its all those vitamins and minerals they take. The Virgo secretary may watch her boss leave his work unfinished and go blissfully out to play golf but she doesn't criticize him. However, she may exude silent disapproval at his retreating back. Overtime poses no problem for Virgos, they would much rather stay until the wee hours and get the job done than worry about it after they get home.

It goes without saying that Virgos need no supervision. The wise boss will allow them as much freedom as possible. They don't like to be watched, it makes them nervous.

Virgo is the fast worker but he seems slow. That is because he goes over every detail with such loving care to make sure it is RIGHT.

If you have a Virgo employee, do not assume that just because he puts in overtime and double checks his work that he is going to be willing to work for you forever at the same job or the same wage. He is well aware of his worth in the current labor market, and he won't hesitate to move if he thinks he's in a dead-end job. Like Cancer, he shares the fear of old age; he will not grow old and have to depend on others for financial help. Curiously, like Capricorn, he seems to retain his youth and health longer than most signs. Even if Virgo is frail as a child he gains health and vigor as he ages. They tend to relax and stop worrying quite so much as they grow older.

The Virgo employee will dress neatly and his office will be painfully orderly. If you see a Virgo looking like a tramp you know there is something seriously wrong. During a real office crisis he assumes a gigantic strength and takes over.

Leos like orange and yellow in their offices. Virgos like soft colors and would prefer their office to be as far away from the typing pool as possible. They get upset if their hours or days off are changed.

You may find a rare Virgo in a creative job such as designing dresses, writing books, or painting pictures, but you can be sure if you look closely that their work is as perfect as they can make it.

Virgos usually get along in a quiet way with most other co-workers. Just stay clear if Sagittarius trips over the phone cord on Virgo's desk and spills coffee on those reports he has just finished.

VIRGO BOSSES

Virgos are only slightly better cut out to be bosses than Pisces. Pisces is acutely miserable in the role of boss most of the time. Virgo sometimes seeks this executive position because of the financial rewards and then discovers he has bitten off more than he can chew. Or possibly he may find himself promoted to the executive suite because he has worked so hard and efficiently at organizing details further down the chain of command. His superiors may have been so impressed with his genius at untangling details they decided to promote him to the executive slot. This often proves a mistake for both management and for the Virgo.

Virgo does organize and untangle, but he doesn't like to do it in the glare of the big office upstairs. The spotlight of the vice presidency shines in his eyes and confuses him. He is trying to sort out details when he should be looking at the big picture. He then may realize he is better suited for a less elevated position. Sometimes he actually wastes his talents as a boss. Not only does he feel uncomfortable but he gets in positions where he tries to cover up his inadequacies by deception. This is a big mistake and is bound to boomerang. He is a terrible and unsuccessful liar. His efforts at fooling people are pathetic.

Another reason for his failure as a boss is his lack of political acumen. When the press or a community committee appears in his office and asks for his opinions he is apt to tell them exactly as he thinks. His frankness is not always expedient and his frantic public relations staff then has to mend his fences.

A Virgo was recently promoted to the head of a governmental agency. Fortunately he doesn't have to entertain his superiors very often. After bitter experience he has learned to curb his tongue and be as diplomatic as possible. If he does have to entertain, he takes his guests to his club for dinner and drinks; this way he can usually keep his foot out of his mouth.

While Virgos are occupying the executive office they frequently spend useless hours worrying about who is tending the store where they used to work. He has trouble delegating responsibilities. If the company is small enough he may be able to do both. If it is too large he will be overwhelmed. If he is going to be successful he will have to learn to concentrate on his own job and leave the details to others, a difficult task for a Virgo.

Virgo will expect his employees to be models of industry. He will not tolerate misspelled words, messy typing or lost invoices and he will know if his employees show up late and leave early. After an employee has offended him twice, he will probably be fired. He will be a very critical boss at best. Neither will he accept criticism from his employees. If he gets a stupid suggestion in his suggestion box he will look for an excuse to dismiss both employee and suggestion.

Men Virgo bosses are as sexy as nature allows them to be but they don't like sex in the business office. Short skirts, braless tops worn by women, or overly tight pants worn by male employees get a cool reception.

Both sexes can be extremely generous with sick leaves for their workers. They understand health problems. They are more human than they appear and can be amazingly kind and generous.

The Virgo boss finds it lonely and scary at the top and sometimes overreacts by being meticulous and picky.

The next time your Virgo boss fuses and fumes over trifles it may help you to understand that at heart he may be very frightened and insecure. This doesn't mean that he is going to change. If you want to continue working for him or her, you had better grin and bear it and put up with the nit-picking. If you happen to be a Virgo yourself you two should understand each other very well. Your fussiness fits. If you are a Leo you probably can't stand him very long. If you are a Cancer you will have to develop a thick skin to let the arrows of criticism fall off without traumatizing you. Scorpios, Capricorns and Taureans will shrug off his pickiness. Aquarians will leave. Aquarius probably would leave that office anyway, Virgo or no Virgo, their field of interest is so divergent. A Pisces simply couldn't stay, he is bleeding. Sagittarius will accept continued reprimands in good grace as long as its fair and all this rain doesn't interfere with Sagittarius' ability to do the job he is paid to do. Aries and Gemini will try to distract the boss by proposing new schemes he can then flesh out with the details. This probably will work and will get Virgo off their backs for a while and give them breathing space.

Whatever you do, if you work for Virgo don't do or say anything he can construe as critical. He is aware of his own shortcomings; he is already worrying about them. Try to smile and go along with him. He does pay you regularly and where could you ever find such good employee sick leave benefit? What if you get clobbered by a beer truck on your way to work?

liBRa
September 22-October 22

HIS ABILITY TO LOVE A WOMAN

Libra is the sign of culture and refinement. His ruling planet is Venus. He is a bit particular about his woman and looks for a lady. If you are a good conversationalist and artist he will be interested. You will not need to have wealthy parents to attract him unless he comes from a wealthy family. He will judge you by his background and standards. Libra is the sign of the Balancing Scales. He is continually weighing and comparing. There may be a rather cool reserve about him, as if he were a spectator of the game of life. However he can have a surprisingly passionate nature. As a lover he is sentimental and vulnerable. He loves to be kissed and petted. Libra is an extremely idealistic sign and is always looking for the ideal woman. When he is aroused he will be tender and gentle. He is not however a verbal lover. Affectionate phrases don't come easily to his lips.

Above all, he will be searching for understanding and sincerity. Petty quarrels are deeply distressing to him. Discord and indifference are most painful because of his intense desire to be in harmony with others, especially you. He will actually try to ignore all forms of ugliness and carefully avoid facing unpleasant situations unless he is forced to do so. He will never overreact to an unpleasant situation; he will simply ignore it.

Since he is so busy considering all sides of the matter, he has a difficult time making up his mind. Sometimes he spends sleepless nights trying to make decisions. Often, he ends up by making no decision at all.

Libras have difficulties making up their minds even as children. Decisions are reached after painful hashing and rehashing of the pros and cons. Sometimes even after a Libra has finally made a decision, he changes his mind.

A woman dating a Libra man will find he is very well organized and makes his plans well in advance. He is in fact very methodical. A typical Libra pattern is found in this example. A Libra had promised to go into partnership in a business venture with a woman friend. They met at lunch and both were bubbling over with plans for the coming purchase. The next thing that happened was he called her and said he had been thinking it over and decided he should "sit on it" for awhile and offered no further explanation. She was deeply hurt and decided he was too unstable to plan any more partnership ventures with. A short time later she ran into him on the street and he smiled that charming, magical smile and she was hooked again. She hasn't written him off entirely, she simply can't; his assets outweigh his faults.

Early in their teens, Libras become interested in women. By the time they get to their twenties they have refined and perfected their romantic techniques. Libra usually gets the girl he chases. Sometimes after he gets her he can't decide if he wants her after all, which can be a bit damaging to the ego of the lady involved. Libras can be fickle and some of them have a curious streak of cruelty. This is often the result of being so terribly busy balancing the scales, their indecision results in cruelty and someone being hurt. Then Libra tries to justify himself but only succeeds in confusing the issue further.

For all their amorous adventures, Libra himself seldom gets hurt. In fact after he has dropped someone he can forget her immediately. If he does suffer a few pangs, no one will ever know.

Libra makes you think he is a fascinating conversationalist. He listens raptly to you, making comments such as "how fascinating, is that really true, I would never have thought that" and you are really flattered. This doesn't mean he is able to relate on a gut level with you, he just sounds like he is. He has found that all these carefully polished and rehearsed tricks make him popular with women.

He loves to debate, sometimes just to hear what you will say. Because he isn't able or willing to get emotionally close to women, trouble often occurs. He won't make any attempts to ferret out hidden motivations. If it isn't on the surface, it isn't important. Although he can't dissect big issues easily, often he can't see what is right under his nose. His ex-girl friends frequently conclude he is a cold and calculating man.

In group situations he charms everyone. He has only to flash that happy, angelic smile and he warms all those in sight. His voice is soft and sweet. He has a way of saying, "you are absolutely right." Then he adroitly presents his argument and before you know what has happened he has won you over to his way of thinking and you have abandoned your own convictions. Sometimes he will argue just to hear your side of the argument. Your Libra is a rather bright man and usually is very good at tactical conversation. He admires clever and intellectual people, especially women.

Depending on the way the scales are tilting, he may be elated or depressed. Usually his mood will change very quickly so if you like him bear with him. Essentially he is a fair man and is remarkably unprejudiced. It is important that you play fair with him. If you do have a difference of opinion he will enjoy discussing it with you. He does, however, have a gift that enables him to induce others to change their minds and to admit they have been mistaken.

A Libra is a very sensitive man, be extremely careful not to slight him. Once he forms a bad impression it usually sticks. He responds best to an atmosphere of quiet, beauty and peace. He is looking for a real soul partner. He will respond to compassion and gentleness. Since he is so sensitive he will take pains not to hurt your feelings because he identifies so easily with you. If he does hurt you, he is generally unaware of it. It is difficult for him to distinguish between flattery and sincere compliments, but make sure you are always sincere. He basks in your approval and your genuine appreciation of what a perceptive fellow he really is. If you can convince him that you are a girl who plays fair, is sympathetic and affectionate, he will date you again and again. A perfect love is what he has been seeking all his life.

RELATIVES

He will not be as interested in his relatives as some of the other signs, Leo for example. He can become quite cool toward any relatives who are dictatorial, especially if they try to tell him how to live his life. He will not get on happily with your relatives if they are careless about their personal appearance or the condition of their homes. If his relatives are people he admires for their fine background he will be quietly proud of them.

MONEY AND CAREER

A Libra man needs financial security to buy the objects of beauty which to him make life worthwhile. Perversely, he sometimes acts as if money grew on trees and spends his capital on possessions when he cannot afford to do so.

Often the Libra man gets what he wants without too much hard work because he is so charming. He has a gift for sales work. He seems to know just what to say to arouse the customer's enthusiasm. He does best at creative work where he can be his own boss. You may, for example, meet your Libra in a museum where he is employed restoring paintings.

He is very intuitive when it comes to making business decisions, and usually his first idea is right. However, he can get into trouble when he tries to rehash his decisions and could end up sitting on the fence. Making decisions is really difficult for him. He has a tendency to drift along unless something really sparks his interest. He is especially good at dealing with ticklish situations in business that require tact and diplomacy. He has a knack of keeping both his customers and his superiors happy. He can often cool a potential hot issue by just chatting rather aimlessly about nothing at all. If he is in one of the service professions such as a barber, head waiter or salesman, he can charm his customers with his rather soothing conversation.

He is an excellent go-between for arbitration in labor-management problems. He can see both sides of the situation and can make each side feel satisfied with the final agreement.

Libra has a rather curious habit of showing apparent impersonality toward people. This is becuase he is really more interested in the situation than the person. It is not that he is cold and calculating, it probably means that his analytical mind is busily at work weighing the pros and cons of the matter.

Since a Libra man must have a fine, elegant home, this often is the motivating factor in his success. Generally, he is a very conservative businessman. However, in a business of his own he is so lacking in aggressiveness and the willingness to take risks he often misses out on money making opportunities. As a partner, he does well when he can work with clients and maintain good will for the business. If he does get involved in a partnership which is not happy for him, he will be the one to break the contract. To him this is the only solution to escape from an atmosphere of inharmony and discord. If he thinks he is being imposed on and is doing more than his share of the work he will end the partnership immediately.

HEALTH AND DIET

His health is moderately strong but is easily affected by his moods. Noise, rudeness and quarrels are traumatic shocks to him. If he becomes depressed he is apt to brood which may bring on a bout of illness. If he becomes upset, rub his back. It will help him to relax.

His skin is somewhat sensitive and rather thin. If on a date you go to the beach, be careful about the amount of sun he gets, even though you think it is not strong enough to burn. He does not tan well, and even when he does get a sort of biscuit color it somehow does not look well on him. If he is not feeling fit, he often breaks out in a rash. He probably does not drink much liquor because he has discovered by now that he cannot tolerate it. Even carbonated drinks are unhealthy for him so have plenty of fresh fruit juice on hand.

He is fond of delicately flavored fish, chicken and lamb dishes. He loves chocolate and may even like to nibble on chocolate brownies in bed.

When he is not feeling well it probably is due to stress or strain of some kind and he has become exhausted. Create a haven of peace and beauty in your home where he can relax under your gentle ministrations.

FRIENDS AND SOCIAL LIFE

Libra enjoys having friends but he is a very discriminating man in his choice of companions. They must be attractive, and oriented to the arts. He can be very critical and intolerante of people he feels are coarse or vulgar in any way. He does best at large social gatherings where he can mix with the people he really enjoys. In a small group he might have a tendency to become overly critical.

CLOTHES HE LIKES TO SEE YOU WEAR

Your Libra man will notice everything you wear. Beauty and grace are closely associated with this sign. He will appreciate the woman who can create the impression of quiet elegance but with just the right touch of a bit of ribbon or lace. Blues and yellows are his favorites, with red and green as second choices. He does not like drab colors, although he admires a sophisticated black accented with a bright color. Fabrics with a sheen, ones that glimmer in soft lights, such as satin or lame, are especially good to wear when he takes you out to dinner.

HOW TO ENTERTAIN A LIBRA

If you have accepted his hospitality many times and have decided you would like to entertain him you might consider an after theatre supper or a musicale at your home. Libras love music and you might discover your special Libran has a lovely voice. He is such a charming man, he has been so thoughtful and considerate and probably has brought you some artistic and beautiful gifts. You want to plan something special that will be just right. Here is a suggestion for your supper:

Cioppino

Garlic Bread   Green Salad

Chocolate Cake

Coffee/Tea

Serve an elegant light, white wine during dinner and follow with his favorite after dinner drink. You can of course vary the menu. Try, however, unless he is allergic, to include chocolate in some form—Libras love it.

WHAT KIND OF HUSBAND WILL HE BE?

Once Libra has decided you are the girl for him he will stop at nothing to get you. His desire for companionship is instinctive and it is very difficult for him to live alone. He knows that in order to live happily he needs a wife. Once married, he will provide you with a beautiful home and will want to help you decorate it. This, of all the signs, is the one most interested in decoration. He has a marvelous sense of color and his ideas are well worth listening to. He may also be very handy at building cabinets and doing some artistic wallpapering. He will want his home to be beautiful and elegant and will spend freely to make it so.

Once you are settled, see to it that his home is run efficiently so that he never sees clutter in the living room, pictures askew, dust on the night table or burned out bulbs in the lamp by his favorite reading chair. He is irritated when there is confusion and noise. Clashing color combinations bother him even when he isn't aware of what is jangling his nerves. Noise and inharmonious colors set the scales off balance. He may react by forgetting to kiss you goodbye in the morning and if his home really gets messy and unkempt he might not come home at all.

Try not to get into arguments with him; let his attempts to involve you in arguments go in one ear and out the other. Love and pet him and show your devotion in a physical way. Make him happy to come home to you and encourage him to bring his friends. He will appreciate a charming, serene hostess and love you forever.

FOODS THAT GRATIFY HIM

A Libra man dearly loves good food and often overindulges in sweets. Rich sauces are really not good for him, but he enjoys them so much! He can be a gourmet. Take care that your meal is served attractively. With this man, "His eye eats first." He will be aware of the color combinations of the food and also of the table setting. Bring out your best silver, lovingly polished to a shining glow, and have the prettiest flower arrangement you can put together on the table. Candlelight and your most elegant hostess gown will complete the picture of dignity, beauty and quiet elegance.

WHAT KIND OF HUSBAND WILL HE BE?

He will not be easy to please. He will like a beautifully decorated home but will not help you with the household chores. If money is limited and you have the choice between a good painting and a refrigerator, be prepared to enjoy the painting.

If he does accumulate money by the time you are married, he will be a very good money manager. Let him handle the finances. He is so anxious to live in a beautiful home that he will budget to make it possible, and do so very carefully. He has an enormous respect for the tradition and sanctity of marriage.

Your Libra man will like to travel and will be bored with too much routine. He will want to take you along on vacation trips so make sure you have the necessary arrangements made so that you can go with him. He will always have an eye for a beautiful woman, but will not stray from your side if you give him a good sex life and an interesting home life. He is a passionate and affectionate man.

WHAT KIND OF FATHER WILL HE BE?

As a father, he will not be too concerned about the health of his children but he will be their charming companion. He has the knack of helping children see beauty through his eyes and he can be an inspiring teacher. He will encourage their interest in the finer things of life. You can take them to the dentist or entertain them at the circus, he is the one who will take them to an art museum and enthrall them with stories about painters and their work. By and large, he will be more attached to you than to his children, but he will love all of you dearly.

LIBRA CO-WORKERS

A Libra employee who found himself in a large, impersonal corporation discovered his office was in a rabbit warren of tiny cubicles. The walls were low enough to see over and he had no privacy. He liked the rest of the set up so he compromised by covering the battleship gray walls with blue wallpaper, bought a soft blue area rug and installed a comfortable easy chair for his clients to sit in. He is the office mediator and under his influence, opposing factions end up shaking hands. His present job may not be his cup of tea but it will do to pay the bills. Libras are able to compromise beautifully. He also exhibits that peculiar quirk of Libra—he never looks angry. He may be angry but he doesn't look it.

Female Libras also decorate their offices artistically. They have a wholesome, outdoors quality that is refreshing. Their voices are sweet and melodious. They are very sexy ladies. Your Libra co-worker or whatever sex will either be married or in the middle of a really heavy affair.

Both sexes like to be surrounded with beautiful things and they are willing to work to achieve them. They don't work harder, they work smarter. They bring to an office their own soothing aura of gentle beauty and peace. Blessed are the peacemakers.

LIBRA BOSSES

If you are a female employee working for a Libra boss you may be half in love with him already, and you don't need to be told how charming he can be. If you are a man you think he is a pretty fair guy. He always listens carefully to both sides of an office dispute and then comes up with a fair decision that somehow manages to please both sides.

Libra moves about the office frequently. You won't find him planted solidly behind his desk Taurean fashion. He moves quickly, but curiously; he never HURRIES. He has the unique quality of moving always at the same speed, as if he was wound up at birth. Nothing varies this metronome like speed. He is seldom late, but he simply doesn't HURRY. People who dash about in a flurry drive him wild.

He is a restless man. He uses the phone a lot and charms people with his sweet voice. He is often out to meetinigs, calling meetings of the office staff and sometimes holding press conferences. Oh yes, this man does reach the heights quite often.

A very successful Libra, quite typical of his sign, prided himself on never having missed a plane, train or bus. He had a plan and he had a backup plan. He had his day scheduled carefully from the time he got up until he went to bed. Sometimes one could sense that decisions were difficult for him but early on he had decided that, in order to be successful and have the luxuries and beauty he craved, he had to master the art of making decisions. Somehow he had been able to stop his scales from teetering back and forth. He of course was and is a highly evolved Libra. Most Libras are very intelligent and if they ever do get to the point of conquering their indecisiveness they are enormously successful bosses, or anything else for that matter.

A less highly evolved Libra may look for an office scapegoat to unload his poor decisions on. Then he will say, "See, you made me do it and it's all your fault." This neatly relieves him of any responsibility. It also puts you in a very untenable position. If you work for a boss who pulls this kind of stunt, be forewarned and keep your mouth shut if you suspect he is trying to maneuver you. Listen carefully to what he says, especially if he prefaces it with, "You are absolutely right."

Both males and females like soft, delicate colors, especially if it is a shade of blue. Both sexes dress beautifully. You never see them showing up in out-of-date or tasteless clothes. Their offices will be softly carpeted and if its a man's office, you can expect to see some artistic nudes. Both sexes like music from opera to the light classics. If things get too topsy-turvy, they settle their nerves with a few minutes quiet or a short nap. Naps are essential to Libras. A short snooze after their rather long lunch charges up their batteries and they can go on late into the night at their same unhurried but distance covering pace.

Women Libras are probably more decisive than men. They have had to learn to make up their minds in order to get to be bosses. A lady Libra who has recently been appointed a judge dispenses justice very carefully after listening to both sides. She is extremely pretty and even prisoners and opposing attorneys can't resist smiling back at her when she turns on the full force of that five hundred watt smile. Judges are often Libras—the scales again.

You will find no stick-in-the-mud resistance toward employee bargaining groups from a Libra boss. He respects the rights of all employes. He won't be threatened or pushed around, either. He will, however, be happy to negotiate the issue.

As bosses, Libras tip their scales from stingy to generous. He may buy a sofa for the women's lounge on Wednesday and then balk at ordering more typing paper. "What happened to all that paper I paid for two years ago?"

All in all, he is a pretty fair boss. Don't let his ups and downs throw you. Who else would compliment you so graciously on the hurry-up typing job you did when he was in such a rush? Who indeed would go to such pains to put scented soap in the rest room just because he wanted to please you? He also could understand why you couldn't stand that dreadful color in your office so he had it repainted. A considerate, friendly and diplomatic boss is the Libra employer.

SCORPIO

October 23-November 21

HIS ABILITY TO LOVE A WOMAN

Your Scorpio man is deep, intense, and probably the most highly sexed man you have ever dated. He is ruled by the planet Pluto. He is not wishy-washy and if he likes you he will pursue your relationship relentlessly. He is a one woman man, while he is dating you, but he likes a little mystery. Hold back a little, if not physically, emotionally. He will. He likes erotic movies and books because they stimulate him. Actually, you will probably decide he really does not need any stimulation. He has some pretty erotic ideas of his own and he will to try them out with you.

He is a very proud man and can also be very stubborn. He has great persistence once he decides on a goal. His lovemaking is intense and he will be totally absorbed. Since his sex drive is so strong he will need a partner who can respond. He needs constant demonstrations of affection. He may be able to read your thoughts and emotions without your telling him. He will have no patience with a woman who is self indugent or lazy, because he himself has so much determination. He will know his own talents as well as his shortcomings and takes care to operate within

83

his limitations. He may impress you as being rather cold and calculating, but beneath this facade there is a great generosity of nature which may surprise you.

He may be rather suspicious of you and he can be very jealous. He does not forget a slight and will devote much time and energy to getting even long after you have forgotten all about it. He is a natural psychologist and usually knows how to induce people to give him what he wants.

He can be very critical, but his criticism is not like that of Virgo.

Scorpios are easy to identify in a crowd. The features are clearly defined and sharp. Sometimes the nose is aquiline. The men usually have a heavy growth of hair. A Scorpio hides his feelings under a mask. He usually wears a poker face, and is so in command of himself he never blushes, seldom frowns, and his smile, though rare, is charming. His eyes have a deep probing intensity. When he stares at you you will look away first, unless you are a Scorpio too. He wants to know all about you—what you are thinking and what your motives are.

He may chatter and joke but don't be fooled. He is watching and observing you closely, just as he is everything around him.

Ancient astrologers refer to the Scorpio sting which was thought to come from serpents. According to the dictionary, Scorpions are "a lobster like arthropod having a poisonous sting." They are capable of stinging themselves to death.

Scorpio is ruled by Mars. Mars lends the traits of aggression and eroticism. Both sexes have compelling sexy voices. Both are noted for tenacity, endurance, over estimation of self, passion and the struggle for survival. Barbault, a famous astrologer, thinks Scorpio is the sexiest sign of the Zodiac. It seems to be true that they can stand sexual excesses which would exhaust natives of other signs. Sexual relationships are powerful driving forces in the Scorpio personality. Scorpio has a tremendously happy sex life or a miserably unhappy one. There seems to be little in between.

Scorpios can be viscious and cunning and they are capable of extreme cruelty in their efforts to get even. They can nurse a grudge for a lifetime until they get their revenge. Scorpios love mysteries and are attracted to the occult. There is nothing superficial about this man; he will tell you what he thinks without any half truths.

He will expect you to meet his emotional needs and to appreciate him. He is looking for his ideal woman who will live with him in his fantasy of the future where there is no loneliness and he is deeply appreciated for what he is. He is willing to work for his future to make his dreams come true. He probably will not confide these dreams to you because he is a rather secretive man. Bide your time and when he is ready to tell you, he will. He is, on the other hand, very curious about the details of your life, especially if he thinks you are seeing another man. He loves gossip. When you first date him he will be out-going and intensely interested in conversation. Suddenly you will realize that he is finding out more about you than you know about him. He really won't tell you much about himself until he feels he knows you better.

He may date you only once and not even call you again if he decides he doesn't like you. He never does things half-way. He doesn't play games. If he does like you, he may demand sex at the end of the first evening together. You are on your own at this point; he is a very determined man.

RELATIVES

Scorpio can be somewhat dictatorial with his relatives because he wants to see them rich and prosperous. He feels responsible for their material success but he probably won't show them much affection. He will tolerate no interference in his personal life from his relatives because he knows how to live his own life. If his parents need his financial help he will be generous with his money up to a point.

MONEY AND CAREER

Your Scorpio man may be somewhat of a gambler. He is apt to play hunches and usually this pays off for him because he is highly intuitive. He is very quick to see opportunities and can make split second decisions. This man could be one of the most successful businessmen you have ever dated. He has a goal, even though he doesn't talk about it to you, and he is pursuing it with great persistence. If one of his plans falls through he will manage to salvage something and continue in pursuit of success.

He is most successful when he is his own boss. He is really too secretive to work well with other people. He sometimes imagines that his co-workers are against him and then he can become a bitter enemy.

He has the gift of being an excellent administrator but he is not fond of menial tasks. In whatever field he enters, he will more than likely be in an executive capacity. Life is a game with him, and money is the way he keeps score. He finds it hard to save money, however; he does have perserverence and seems to accumulate money in spite of himself. When he does get some money he makes it grow. If he owns property he is very good at managing it so it increases greatly in value.

Sometimes he makes mistakes because he is over confident and gets carried away with his plans, especially if he has gambled for high stakes. You may hear him talk of his luck, but even though luck is of some importance to him underneath it all there is much skill and cunning.

As in everything else he does, Scorpio sets himself a goal and there are no halfway measures. His creative urge drives him to be successful. He is a powerful person, a doer and an achiever. More than any other sign, he is a self starter. His work is more important to him than anything; he is his work.

HEALTH AHD DIET

A Scorpio man is seldom ill because he takes such good care of himself. He if he does fall prey to whatever bug is going around he keeps going because he doesn't like to admit that he is really ill. How can he be sick when he has so many projects to complete? If he is convinced he needs medical help he will see a doctor at once. Hard physical exercise is good for him.

FRIENDS AND SOCIAL LIFE

He likes to entertain his friends, but for some reason does not really get involved with them. He has a rather impersonal feeling about people but he admires the successful ones. If he is offended by his friends he can be quick to lash out at them. If he is really wounded by friends he will bide his time until he can get his revenge. Most people give Scorpio a wide berth after he has attacked them and never really trust him again. He can become a fearful enemy because he doesn't forget, even after others have.

CLOTHES HE LIKES TO SEE YOU WEAR

This man has some very definite ideas of what kind of clothes he likes to see women wear. He admires clothes that are chic, not mod, ladylike, not flashy. Sexy underthings intrigue him, like leopard panties and red slips. His tastes are sophisticated and erotic. Heavy exotic perfume is good, but it has to be expensive, he can tell. Avoid costume jewelry at all costs. Even a smaller insignificant piece of real jewelry will catch his eye and his appreciation. He's very apt to give you a gift of pearls or some attractive semi-precious stone.

HOW TO ENTERTAIN SCORPIO

The Scorpio you are dating is very likely to be interested in sports. He may belong to the Sierra Club, a biking club, or he may just like to get out in the back country on weekends. Scorpios are physically strong and like to stretch their muscles in the outdoors. If he invites you on a hike, offer to bring the food. This menu might please Scorpio:

Small Canned Ham
Potatoes to fry or bake in Coals
Sliced Tomatoes in Dill Weed   Cornbread with Honey
Fruit and Cookies with Coffee or Tea

Buy a small canned ham to slice and heat in a mini fry pan. You can partially cook the potatoes at home then wrap them in foil to finish baking in campfire coals. Make cornbread ahead of time and get some rich chewy cookies from the bakery. This menu doesn't require a lot of supplies to carry. You will need only two utensils to cook with, the fry pan and a pot for coffee.

If your Scorpio is a fisherman, take along some cornmeal and cooking oil for the fish and lemons to squeeze over his catch. Have fun!

FOODS THAT GRATIFY HIM

He knows all about balanced diets and is partial to high protein foods. Broil him a lobster without a sauce, or a big juicy steak rare. Serve a simple salad. Though he is apt to change his food preferences frequently, he usually wants meat and potatoes. He has strong likes and dislikes. He probably is rather a fast eater and doesn't like interruptions during the meal.

WHAT KIND OF HUSBAND WILL HE BE?

Your Scorpio husband will want to possess you and sexual fulfillment will be the basis for his possessiveness. If he is sexually frustrated he will not be happy and though he may give you other reasons, the real trouble will be sex. He can become very bitter if this happens. He can be very jealous of you, take care you don't provoke his jealousy because he is slow to forgive. He can be very moody and not know himself why this occurs. He will also be very intuitive about your moods. He seems to sense the cause of your tensions and anxieties without your telling him. You may expect him to be very critical of you, but unlike the criticism of a Virgo, he will criticize you constructively.

A Scorpio man will often marry for money or position. He is very proud and he likes material possessions. He will provide a comfortable home and expect you to manage it efficiently. He will resent it if you allow the mechanics of running a house to interfere with living. Try to keep the home operating smoothly without bothering him with the nitty-gritty details. A Scorpio man does not take kindly to fussing with a stopped up sink. He somehow feels he is above all that nonsense.

He will wake you early and expect you to be up with him so he can have his morning coffee with you. He likes to be up early because he has so many half-finished projects bubbling away. He doesn't need as much sleep as most people. He feels sleep is rather a waste of time. He is a cheerful fellow in the morning, one that is pleasant and interesting to be with.

If you try to dominate him you will have a rocky marriage. He just does not understand domineering women. He is a natural leader and will expect you to defer to his wishes.

If you can create a relationship that will satisfy his deep need for sexual fullfilment you will have a happy marriage. If he attains a good sex life with you he will feel he has been successful in one of the most important areas of his life. He will not stray from you. Why should he? You will have made him very happy. He is really a one woman man. Unfortunately, if you become offhanded about the importance of sex in the marriage you may lose him, no matter what his age. He is always aware of the sexual attraction of other women. If this does happen, he will not attempt to deceive you. He will tell you. As his wife you will have all the advantages against the other women, so spend some of your spare time thinking up new tricks to fascinate him.

WHAT KIND OF FATHER WILL HE BE?

He will provide his children with all that they need in the way of material comforts. His attitude toward his children may be rather impersonal. He will expect you to assume the details of their care. He is more devoted to you because he knows they will leave the home and you will remain. You are tremendously important to him, more important than his children.

SCORPIO CO-WORKERS

The ruthlessness, determination and control which appears so strongly in the Scorpio boss is strangely missing in the employee. By now you have probably done a little sleuthing (if you are interested in the people you work with) and have spotted several Scorpio employees. You probably think they are the exception to the rule. The attractive brunette with the flashing smile and ladylike manner who would never lose her cool, can she really be a Scorpio? She is so kind and accommodating. You can't imagine her plotting to get someone's job and she doesn't seem to have made any enemies in the entire office. If you describe her to someone you may think of "tranquil." She has typed a letter over four times for the boss because he kept changing his mind, but she keeps on smiling. She patiently sat through a staff meeting taking notes and, in front of her co-workers, her boss criticized her (her boss is a fussy afflicted Cancer). Does she stalk out in a huff? Not this lady.

Take a good look. You are watching a pre-boss Scorpio getting to the executive lounge. She will be accommodating and patient and never take offense at rude remarks from her boss. Her stakes are high. Also, she thinks that since she is working for the man and taking his money he has the right to treat her any way he likes, rudely or not. You will note that she will probably treat her underlings the same way. She is well aware of the privileges of rank.

A male Scorpio employee plays the same game. There is the story of a male Scorpio who worked for an agricultural chemical company as a salesman selling farm chemicals to feed and seed dealers. His territory encompassed two western states. Since he was a newcomer on the sales staff it was his job to find customers who had not previously dealt with this particular firm. He went out "cold turkey" and was very successful in recruiting customers. He made significant sales, all the more surprising since there were other chemical companies covering the same areas. He weaned customers away from the competition by the sheer force of his personality. When he returned to the office after a week on the road he discovered that his boss had cancelled some of the orders he had sold because he couldn't deliver. His boss had neglected to tell him this before he left. His boss had also neglected to tell him he was taking the week off to sail in a race. He couldn't even discuss the problem with him, he wasn't there. Can you guess his reaction? He simply called his secretary in, made a precise report of his customer contacts with suggestions for their future needs and left the finished memorandum on his bosses' desk. Perfect control, no one knew he was upset. You see, there was a vice-presidency opening up in this firm which is why he had come to work there in the first place. He was laying careful plans for this position. Meanwhile he would take what came with no complaints. He was already planning his next move.

SCORPIO BOSSES

Watch your step with Scorpio. He is patient, loyal, generous, sympathetic and courteous until he is angry. There is no fury like a Scorpio. The Taurean's bellow is nothing compared to this volatile sign. He not only gets angry and shouts he gets sarcastic as well. He can lose all appreciation for the sensibilities of his employees.

He is always suspicious. He will condemn his employees for doing exactly what he does himself. You may already have been stung by Scorpio if you work for one and he caught you coming in late or making a stupid mistake. There is not much that escapes his attention.

If you ask him for a favor he will either reply promptly, "Yes, of course," or turn you down flatly, and that decision is final. You've got to be pretty tough to work for Scorpio. He doesn't care what his employees think of him.

On the other side of the coin, when times are hard and other businesses are folding up, Scorpio pitches in and works harder than ever before to keep his company solvent. He never expected to get something for nothing and never feels sorry for himself. He may make scathing remarks in staff meetings to shake up his employees and then privately tell them if he thinks they are doing a good job. He knows what kind of work they are doing because he watches them closely.

If he likes you, and he probably does or he wouldn't have hired you, he can suddenly become sympathetic when you least expect it. It's as if Dracula suddenly brought you flowers. He will flash his rare smile and you realize he is a great guy to work for, maybe even a sweet and thoughtful one. Not true. Sweet he isn't. But he isn't Dracula either. He expects total loyalty from his employees and anything less is grounds for immediate dismissal. Never try to calm him down with false flattery, he will see through you in an instant.

You couldn't ask for a more courageous, determined employer. He understands business trends and he understands people.

Women Scorpio bosses are pretty much the same as their brother Scorpios. They too are strikingly handsome and sharp featured. Sometimes the women have photogenic bone structure and beautiful cheek bones. Katherine Hepburn is an example. The lady Scorpio is secretive and never exposes her deepest feelings around an office and seldom to her close friends. She can be unpredictable and when aroused can fail to see anyone's viewpoint but her own. Her office will reflect her intense desire for prestige. She knows she is good and expects everyone else to know it too. She does not know the meaning of humility.

Scorpio, according to most astrologers, is a faithful employee and will work overtime. Some Scorpios, mainly the women, however, will not deign to work overtime in anybody's office and are quite clever in escaping this task. They are extremely verbal and can screech like a fishwife if an employee angers them (somewhat like a fussy Virgo). They are capable of overwhelming opposition and will scheme and maneuver their way to an executive position where they will then do an outstanding job.

Most of the time your Scorpio boss will have himself under total control and run his company, plant, or whatever more efficiently than most signs. He knows exactly where he is going and how to get there. Perhaps the Scorpio has earned a rather undeserved negative reputation through bad 'public relations.' People he has stung remember him for the painful sting; they tend to forget his qualities of superior ability, loyalty, courage and a good many other talents that are there if you look for them.

SAGITTARIUS

November 22-December 21

HIS ABILITY TO LOVE A WOMAN

Your Sagittarius date will be outgoing, friendly, and very, very charming. He has the patent on charm.

Sex can be a game with him, and a rather intense game at that. He likes to flirt, but is difficult to trap. He thinks he is a sex expert but he may actually be a bit clumsy. He is a very direct and outspoken individual about everything, including sex, and if you approach him in the direct way he approaches you you will communicate very well. If he hurts your feelings tell him so.

He does not like phony, insincere girls and is quite clever at spotting them. Don't lie to him, this will shock and hurt him. How could you lie to such a sincere fellow? Sincere or not, his attention span may be rather short, so remember the game part. He does like his freedom, and if he has not married yet, this is probably why.

Your dates may be mostly outdoor activities, at least at the start. He loves fresh air and sports of all kinds. Unlike Scorpio, he revels in group sports.

He is a very idealistic man, and strives for perfection in everything he does. Sometimes he holds back fearing that he can't achieve perfection.

Sagittarius is the sign of the philosopher and he constantly asks himself questions and speculates on the answers. He is an abstract thinker and probably reads a great deal. It would behoove you to bone up on some of the writings of the philosophers, contemporary and ancient. If you can bat the conversational ball back to him with some intelligent comments of your own, he will be fascinated. He likes intelligent women. He does not like idle gossip; it bores him.

He is one of the most curious men you will ever date. He will want to know all about your beaux, past and present, and will ask very direct questions. Be a trifle mysterious, don't satisfy his curiosity. Occassionally let him wonder where you were. Try to come up with some interesting new projects of your own that will keep you happily occupied when he isn't around. He may *not* be around as much as you would like—he can change his moods very suddenly. Just when you think he is interested he may not show up for awhile. However, if he says he will call you, he will. He believes in keeping his word. And, by the same token, he will expect you to keep yours. Just don't let him become too sure of you and remember that his freedom is very precious to him.

If he seems attractive to you, you may have to push through the crowd to get to him in the beginning. He has so many friends. He may also have a mistress tucked away, but he somehow takes a long time getting around to marriage. Women often mistake his flirtations for something more serious. He can look like a little lost boy who needs some mothering. He is only looking for a gal to pal around with. If the girl becomes overly possessive he simply fades away unless, and this is important, she has been a good stimulating companion, not only sexually but intellectually and mentally.

You will see him flirting with the waitress, the lady cab driver, any female who takes his fancy when you go out together. He can't help it. It is best to curb your jealousy and give him lots of leeway. You can definitely scare him off in the early stages of your friendship if he thinks you are going to inhibit his freedom. That doesn't mean you must be a doormat or pine away for his attention. Develop lots of interests of your own and you won't be hanging around the phone every night waiting for him to call. Let him know that you value your freedom also; yours is a full and busy life. If and when he gets around to telling you he thinks you are all he has ever wanted, tell him you think he is great too and you have always been curious about what it would be like to be married or have children. He will respect your desire for adventure. You must polish up a few special talents to hold him. he will want to show you off to his many friends who will be interesting, successful people.

Be honest with him, he is capable of quick anger and can be physical if you goad him too far. His emotions sometimes rule his head. He is just letting off steam and the outburst will be over as quickly as it started. Don't play games with him and remember he isn't easy to capture.

RELATIVES

He is moderately attached to his relatives. He wants to be proud of them and if they are interesting to him he will spend time with them. He will also point out their mistakes in a rather blunt manner. He will attend family reunions and spend holidays with them only if he thinks their company will be more interesting than that of his friends. He will not let his relatives impose on him.

MONEY AND CAREER

He is a born optimist and can be successful in almost any field that offers challenge and variety. His work frequently involves travel. He will avoid any job that means punching a time clock or one that seems to lead nowhere. Being an optimist, he continually expects good things to happen to him and somehow they do. He is especially qualified when it comes to managing property and commodities. He seems to learn early in life how to acquire the money to buy the things he wants. He may have a good many more assets than you think he has, he is a pretty shrewd businessman. He has a great deal of rather casual patience and can wait a long time for business deals to work out for him, and of course they usually do.

He may be involved in humanitarian work of some kind. He is often deeply religious and feels that business should benefit others as well as himself.

He will never starve nor will his bills go unpaid. Money, to him, is for spending and he can be a rather impulsive spender. In all his business dealings he is scrupulously honest and straightforward.

HEALTH AND DIET

He is such an active man he sometimes forgets to eat. If he is involved with a friend or a business associate he probably won't even think about food. He isn't much of a gourmet. He likes alcohol and can drink more than some of the other signs without showing any dissipation. Too much liquor makes him gain weight, especially around the hips and stomach. Then he will exercise at some of his beloved sports and the fat will just seem to melt off. Because of his somewhat tender skin, he may sunburn easily. He may lose his hair from overexposure to hot, dry winds and too much sun. Generally, he has good health to an old age.

FRIENDS AND SOCIAL LIFE

He is a gadabout and so are his friends. He loves to have friends in for dinner and good conversation. If they bore him he might drop them quite suddenly. He has very strong convictions and is a vigorous defender of the underdog. That doesn't necessarily mean he agrees with him, but he will defend him if he thinks he is being treated unfairly. He is sensitive to injustice. He believes the best of people and fairly sparkles with good will and faith.

CLOTHES HE LIKES TO SEE YOU WEAR

He will prefer you to wear smartly cut sports clothes that are dashing and a little different. Casual and expensively simple styles appeal to him. If he arrives at your door on the spur of the moment with a suggestion for an outing, he won't appreciate being kept waiting while you fiddle with an elaborate costume. Come on as a healthy, outdoor girl who looks as if she wore no makeup at all, which will mean, of course, your spending more time achieving your "no makeup look." He knows that you wear makeup, of course, but he doesn't like gobs of goo and hairpieces that come off in the pool. Since you will be spending much of your time involved in sports, take pains to keep appropriate outfits at hand so you will be ready at a moment's notice. He won't give you much warning, even after you're married. He is especially fond of blues and turquoises. Way out peignoires and sexy nightgowns delight him.

HOW TO ENTERTAIN YOUR SAGITTARIUS

Sagittarians love sports of all kinds. Horse races, football, baseball, hockey, bullfights. One of your first dates might be to the football or baseball game, depending on the season. If he does invite you to a game suggest a tailgate party and you provide the goodies. You might suggest that he invite some of his friends and you can all gather for a picnic before the game. He will probably be enthusiastic and pleased that you thought of a treat for him and his friends. Here is a sample menu for a tailgate picnic:

Sloppy Joes on Hamburger Buns

Crock Pot Baked Beans   Potatoe Salad

Three Bean Salad   Relishes

Apple Pie and Cheeses for Desert

Plan carefully so that foods will be served at their tastiest temperatures. Pre-cook the sloppy joes and keep them warm in a crockery dish wrapped in newspaper, unless you can manage a sterno can to heat them in. Bring sturdy eating equipment that can be thrown away and although they aren't necessary, camp stools or folding chairs are a nice addition for everyone's comfort, he probably has a supply in his garage since he does enjoy camping out.

If your friend is a sailor you can use the same menu. For a picnic in the mountains take along a portable barbecue and barbecue steaks instead of the sloppy joes. If you are on a picnic be sure to take along a soft ball or some other sports equipment he might enjoy playing with.

If he is a fisherman plan a fishfry with sliced fried potatoes, sourdough bread heated on the grill in foil, salad, and plenty of lemon juice or tartar sauce for the fish. For this, a red checked tablecloth would be fun and plenty of pillows for lounging after he has enjoyed your delicious cooking.

Sagittarians don't usually have any particular hangups about drinking and alcohol doesn't bother them physically. I would suggest beer for the tailgate party kept well chilled. He and his friends may prefer something like bloody mary's and you can check with him on this. He will enjoy planning the outing and helping you with the supplies.

FOODS THAT GRATIFY HIM

Deliciously flavored sauces are not his dish. Fix him spicy and exotic foods. He likes pastrami sandwiches that you can prepare when the mood strikes him. Keep a liberal supply of wines and after dinner drinks on hand. He won't like to be kept waiting if he is invited to your home for dinner, so keep the cocktail hour short.

WHAT KIND OF HUSBAND WILL HE BE?

He may be casual about his friends, but never about his wife. He will put her on a pedestal. Once he has made his choice, he will tend to idealize his wife and somehow never seem to see her faults. He will be friendly rather than overly affectionate. As a married man, he may indulge in mild flirtations but he is a strong believer in the tradition of marriage and his affairs are not serious. He will never allow an affair to interfere with his marriage. He is a transparent liar and if you guess what is going on and confront him with it he will not lie to you. Unless he feels that you are interfering with his cherished freedom he will be a very loyal husband. Be careful that you don't overreact to his flirtations, it may be just spontaneous friendliness on his part. He can be very impulsive but not if he thinks it may jeopardize his home.

Your home with your Sagittarius husband will have sparkle and good will. He will be an excellent host and you will do a lot of entertaining. He will have some clever decorating ideas of his own and will want to help you with your decorating schemes. You may not spend as much time in your home as you would be spending with Pisces, Taurus or Capricorn because he will want to travel and he will want you by his side to share all his enthusiasms.

WHAT KIND OF FATHER WILL HE BE?

As he is never casual about his wife, your Satittarius husband will not be casual about his children either. He will take a very sober and dedicated attitude toward them. He will be honest and direct in his dealings with his children and will tolerate nothing less from them. He will instill his religious values in his children. He will encourage them to read and to question. Higher education is very important to him and he will encourage his children to go to college.

SAGITTARIUS CO-WORKERS

Women Sagittarians have a most unusual trait that may drive their co-workers frantic. Women of this sign are almost always uncoordinated to the point they trip over their own feet, knock over piles of papers someone else has just carefully collated, and generally seem like bulls in a china shop. Its not that they are consciously destructive or aggressive, they just simply move fast and things seem to get in their way. They are the sort of person who is frequently tripping over their own feet. In rapid succession they might manage to shut their thumb in the car door, slip and sprain a leg, and you always expect them to suffer some other accident any moment. Men seem to be less accident prone than women in the sign of Sagittarius.

Both sexes are very conscientious workers and simply cannot let their work slide. They will stay as late as necessary to get their assignments completed. Honesty is very important to them and they will willingly go to bat for another employee they think is being victimized. The archer is brutally honest at times. He or she says what is what, and lets the chips fall where they may. You may occasionally find a Sagittarian who has been exposed to the chain of command in an organization, such as the military, long enough to have learned diplomacy, but this is rather rare. They usually are frank and honest to the extreme and rather enjoy telling others what to do. Don't brush them off, they are usually very perceptive. Most archers have an uncanny ability to brush aside nonessentials and get to the heart of problems very quickly. You will seldom see one bogged down with details so he or she can't see the forest for the trees. Details bore archers. Once they set their mind on a goal they dive in and take on the most perplexing problems, confident in the knowledge that they are going to win. Usually they do win. The Jupiter luck seems to follow them all their lives and if they listen to their hunches they come out on top. Fortunately archers seem to sense this; they don't listen to other people too often. The archer secretary may often spill her bosses' coffee on her or on him but she has such a cheerful, sparkling personality no one seems to mind. Sometimes some of her bloopers turn out to be blessings in disguise. The telephone order she didn't place turns out to have been to the company which went into receivership the next week. The customer she served coffee to and chatted with out of politeness because she felt sorry for him waiting so long to see the boss is actually a millionaire wearing shoes and suits from Sears Roebuck. She has a way of getting people to respond to her and they tell her things they probably haven't even told their best friends. She is not a gossip and secrets are respected.

Sagittarians love to travel and if they find themselves in a selling job which involves trips they are usually happy. They will get restless in routine jobs. He or she may be a bit impulsive, dashing out to sell his customers, but again the Jupiter luck rescues him from his blunders and he comes back to the office a happy employee.

Most archers are very curious and like to know what is behind the orders they are being given. They aren't thrown by changes in office procedure but they do like to know the whys and wherefores. In fact, they are curious about everything that goes on in the office. If the Pisces employee is the last to hear the latest news, the archer is the first. They always have the knack for being where the action is.

In addition, there is nothing small or petty about Sagittarians as employees. Their grand gestures, acts of generosity, and supreme optimism are sure to cheer up any office. They are good for office morale and good for the customers.

SAGITTARIAN BOSSES

The archer boss is not like a Capricorn or Scorpio or Taurus. These signs usually run their offices with compulsive precision. He is a little like a Gemini, but not quite. Sagittarians run their offices with a loose rein and on the surface office procedures appear to be rather slipshod. Look again. He knows he is allergic to details so he is smart enough to hire others to take over these chores for him. He sees no sense in cluttering up his mind with information he can pay others to give him. He will have a good bookkeeper, and will trust him to keep track of expenses. His employees know he is in business to make a profit. He is the idea man and leaves details to others.

Sales meeting with the archers are lively and frank. He may burst out with a candid but funny summation of the salesman who blew the deal that was so important to the company and will join in the laughter. Then he will say something like, "You do things that annoy me but whatever your faults you are honest, and we admire you for it." Honesty is important to him. He is honest, brutally so, but his employees can't stay mad at him for long. They may feel like clobbering him one minute, but will want to kiss him the next. He has few inhibitions and loves to correct other people's mistakes. He gives orders with the regal air of the Leo but is more jovial than Leo. He is sometimes tactless but somehow his employees find it easy to forgive him. Perhaps because he himself is so forgiving and fair.

Tactless he may be, awkward to the point of stumbling over the telephone cords, but dull witted he is not. He may take the up elevator when he means to go down, but he can run his business with a superb organization and a mind for priorities. His ideas are often ahead of his competitor's ideas by a country mile, again, thanks to the Jupiter luck and intuition. He is a study in contrasts and the longer you work for him the more surprised you will be about him. Just when you think you have him figured out he will display another facet of his character.

He is very fair about vacations, time off, and will be generous with bonuses. He will expect you to be fair with him. He does not know how to deal with dishonesty, prevarications and hypocrisy. Be fair with him in all your dealings; give him a day's work for a day's pay and enjoy being part of his office. Whatever else, it won't be dull!

CAPRICORN
December 22-January 19

HIS ABILITY TO LOVE A WOMAN

Your Capricorn man is a very well organized, solid citizen. He is a little embarrassed about any sexual silliness. He is a very proper man and will initiate his lovemaking with carefully chosen gifts. A beautifully bound volume of Shakespeare with a discreet card, or a dozen perfect red roses on the anniversary of your meeting, for example. He desperately needs appreciation and encouragement. The woman who makes him feel that he is a successful man who has arrived, at least with her, can lead him easily.

Even though he is a little stuffy about the sexual side of your relationship, he will try anything. Be a little unconventional, he likes to master whatever he does. He thinks he should get to know you better. All of this is in the interest of furthering his education, of course.

This man knows just where he is going and how he is going to get there. Sometimes he takes two steps only to fall back one. Capricorn is ruled by Saturn, the planet of limitation and fear. He always feels its stern limitations and never knows the exhilaration of being truly free. He somehow becomes accustomed to this constant limitation and adapts himself. He learns he frequently has to stop and consolidate his gains before going on. He is an extremely ambitious man and wants to get to the top for the fame and fortune it will bring him. He misses many joys of today because he is so intent on tomorrow. Step by step he will achieve his goals and he feels a deep need for a wife who can help him. He is not above marrying for money for he is a realist. If he is dating you at all by now, he has probably checked you out pretty thoroughly. You likely have similar backgrounds and have many tastes in common. He does not marry hastily. Marriage, after all, is another of the ambitions he wants to satisfy and he will find a suitable wife with the same methodical approach he uses in business.

You may feel he is becoming too possessive too soon, and you may feel that he could become very jealous. You could be right. He may be very undemonstrative on the surface, but he really craves love and affection. He is ill at ease in emotional situations. He covers his deep feelings with bright chatter. He is somewhat fearful of revealing how deeply he may love you until he is very sure you will not reject him. Even when he is sure of your love he will not often tell you he loves you. He will show you by his care and concern for your well being and, on appropriate occasions, with thoughtful gifts.

One of this man's unique traits is his habit of answering a question with a question. This can be maddening for you, but is part of his character that will not change, so you should learn to live with it if you want him.

Your Capricorn man needs a woman who is warm and understanding, and incidentally, one who can teach him a few things about sex. If he really likes you and finds that you satisfy these basic needs you will have a very devoted man. He does like to take care of those he loves.

If you happen to need help in some typical single girl crisis, such as a ride to your doctor's office for an eye test, call on your Capricorn. He likes to feel needed. In any emergency he is a Rock of Gibraltar because he doesn't get rattled. He has a genius for bringing order out of chaos and he can see the big picture.

Since his greatest fear is the unknown, don't try to make him jealous by playing little tricks on him, you will only convince him that he can't depend on you.

He isn't much for spur of the moment entertainment, either he likes to plan ahead and make reservations or set up a well planned guest list. He will take you to good restaurants and the evening will be carefully arranged. If you are a bit uninhibited yourself you may think your Capricorn is a pretty rigid, compulsive man. It helps to have a clear understanding of his needs. He has had to work very hard for everything he has and sometimes he may decide that it is his lot in life to suffer. He feels great despair when he fails, even temporarily. Try to build up his faith in himself.

Some Capricorn men like to manage other people's lives. They are born organizers. Don't be surprised if he tries to manage yours. He may have some very practical ideas. Let him help you when he can, this makes him feel protective, which he likes.

Your Capricorn won't talk about his plans, he believes in showing the world tangible results. Then you will see him at his best, a man of quiet dignity and restraint.

RELATIVES

A Capricorn man may like to manage the lives of his relatives. He will care for them if they are in need of his help and they know they can depend on him. He is very loyal to his family. His elderly parents will never want for any creature comforts if he can possibly afford it. He feels this is his duty, however, he is not very sentimental about his relatives.

MONEY AND CAREER

Your Capricorn has his eye on prestige and status in his community. He is a hard worker and since he is so often delayed by Saturn he is a very determined worker. He has to be, because if he doesn't have enough money to tide him over in an emergency he is miserable. He always feels that the inevitable rainy day is coming and he intends to be prepared.

In business he does well as long as he can run things himself. He is not a very understanding boss and has little patience with his employees' problems. Sometimes he belittles his employees. He almost never becomes involved with them personally.

He is very honest and fair with others in his business dealings. He likes to see others get ahead if they are able. He is not very competitive himself, and he expects to get ahead by sheer hard work and persistence.

He probably has a good insurance policy and sizable investment in property not affected by inflation. He doesn't gamble in any business. You can expect him to acquire quite a bit of the world's goods by the time he is ready to retire. Many millionaires are Capricorns.

Your Capricorn will do very well in any business where he can give his debtors every chance to get on their feet before collecting from them.

Good ethics are important to him and he may talk to you about the responsibilities of wealth. Cary Grant, Howard Hughes, Abe Lincoln and Barry Goldwater are Capricorns.

A typical Capricon rarely overindulges in anything. He can be particular about food and his likes and dislikes are quite definite. He may not like very spicy or highly seasoned food. You don't need to be a gourmet cook to please him. The old standbys his mother served him, such as scalloped potatoes, pot roast, strawberry shortcake made with rich biscuits, are especially good. Try to find out the dishes his mother served that he particularly liked, he will be pleased. You may get the feeling he is checking you out as a wife and a hostess. He is. Have plenty of catsup, salt and pepper so he can make everything taste familiar.

FRIENDS AND SOCIAL LIFE

His friends will tend to be rather sober, hardworking people. He is far too serious to enjoy small talk at a cocktail party. He will choose his friends carefully and you may think he sometimes gets carried away with those who have the status and influence he himself is seeking. Certainly, many of his friends will be wealthy, influential people and this didn't happen by accident. There can be a ruthlessness in his makeup that keeps him from getting really involved with anyone. He can discard a loyal friend if he feels that he has been outgrown. He can also be suspicious and he rarely confides in people. He may tell you frankly that he doesn't really trust people. Believe him.

CLOTHES HE LIKES TO SEE YOU WEAR

He will be shocked if you wear any costume that makes you conspicious. You can wear anything sexy, but be subtle. A navy blue dress with a white collar that is just a bit low, but not obviously low. Black dresses with well cut lines are good. He especially likes the type of black dress that has chiffon sleeves and a high neck that you can see through. Sexy, but proper. Just take care to be suitably dressed for every occasion, which shouldn't be too difficult. He will give you plenty of advance notice about the plans he has made.

HOW TO ENTERTAIN YOUR CAPRICORN

Since he does not like frantic, jammed cocktail parties or hordes of people, and is acutely uncomfortable in nightclubs or discoteques, try cooking him a homey, old fashioned dinner like his mother might have prepared. In fact, it might be a nice beginning to your dinner invitation to inquire what his mother did cook and which of all her dishes he especially liked. You may be sure he remembers, he was probably underfoot much of the time he was growing up, watching her cook. Here is a suggestion you might like to start with:

Old Fashioneds
Cheeses, Fresh Vegetables such as Carrots,
Zucchini, Cucumbers, Cut in Sticks
Dip of your Choice
Pot Roast with Carrots, Potatoes,
Onions in Rich Brown Gravy
Hot Biscuits, Honey, Butter
Home Made Ice Cream (Vanilla),   Hermit Cookies

As you can see, there is nothing unfamiliar or strange, and it will keep on the back burner in case his hectic office schedule necessitates a delay. The home made ice cream is a nice, old fashioned touch and not too difficult to manage with an electric freezer. How many girls does he know, for goodness sake, who would have the perception and the wit to entertain him in this manner?

For your next venture with him, you might try a conventional sit down dinner with carefully chosen couples who are successful in some form of business venture, and if, by a bit of luck, are also tuned in to some art form, "Voila." He will see you are not only a superb cook, capable of entertaining him well, but you also are a gracious hostess who could welcome to his home the people he enjoys. You are on your way.

A sample menu for this dinner might be as follows:

Coleslaw
Baked Ham
Baked Red Apples
Baked Scalloped Potatoes
Home Made Bread, Rolls, or Cornbread
Lemon Pie

Make sure you have a good supply of a variety of liquors on hand plus a set of rather heavy cut glass glasses if you can afford them. In fact, make sure you have as nice accessories as possible, never mind if they have been handed down from Aunt Minnie and grandmother. If they are silver or pewter, polish them up and use them with pride. With Capricorn, old is better. If you know the history of any of your pieces he will be interested in hearing about them. Don't forget his reverence for tradition.

If his mother or father are living nearby, invite them over. He will love you for it. Make sure the invitation is casual and non-threatening so that he can't misconstrue your intentions, like lassoing him at the end of the dessert course. You will have to use your own intuition for this. He does tend to be suspicious. Keep your hippie brother, the one who smokes pot, far away when you entertain the Capricorn. Seeing you with questionable persons will not earn you Brownie points.

Let him see you in your own home, surrounded by your own well cared for possessions, serene, warm and ladylike, attentive to his needs. He admires order and serenity, and of course you epitomize all that he admires.

FOODS THAT GRATIFY HIM

Your Capricorn will enjoy hot coffee, broths, rare steaks and home-made brownies. When he gets depressed he often gets cold and his muscles tighten. If you have a fireplace so much the better. When he arrives tired and tense from the battles of the day, suggest that he let you massage his neck and back. Massage really helps to unwind him so that he can relax and appreciate wonderful, sexy you, and later, the dinner you have been keeping warm in the oven.

WHAT KIND OF HUSBAND WILL HE BE?

Your Capricorn has set very high goals for himself and this also applies to marriage. If he thinks he isn't doing too well at the moment in his role of husband he can become stubborn and moody. He can sometimes be just plain mean. Always remember that he craves love and affection, and most of all, reassurance, even when he isn't acting like he does. His morale needs continual bolstering. If you don't build him up he can be attracted to another wise women who will. If you make him feel truly appreciated and secure, he will be more apt to show the deep love that he has for you. He probably won't stray if he really loves you as long as you don't forget how to handle him. He may expect you to run a very tight ship and account for every cent he gives you. Essentially, though, he is a very loyal husband.

The home he provides you will be comfortable and traditional, and he will want to do a lot of entertaining. He knows that he can accomplish more business at a dinner table than at the office. He will want to impress his business associates and will expect you to be a gracious hostess. In order to pass inspection with him, his home should be perfect in every detail. He will happily spend the money to make his home as elegant as he feels it should be.

He may be an unforgiving husband if you have an extra-martial affair. Some Capricorns do not believe in second chances for anyone, not even a wife. If you are so careless as to bring disgrace upon him as a result of your indiscretion, he will never be able to forgive you and your marriage will end.

As his wife, you will be expected to assume the managerial responsibilities of the home so that he can devote his time to his business. Make sure that you keep your household accounts in good order so that he does not have to be at all concerned with the actual running of the home. He will see that you have sufficient funds to manage the home properly and will hire a handy-man or repairman to keep things running smoothly.

WHAT KIND OF FATHER WILL HE BE?

As a father he will be concerned with the welfare of his children, but he may equate love with money. That is, he will see that they have all the comforts and luxuries they need, but he may be rather undemonstrative with his children and have difficulty communicating with them. He craves love and affection but his children may not realize how deeply he loves them. He will be a stickler for discipline. He will attempt to instill good moral values in his children and will expect them to be honest with him. His children can count on his financial help even after they leave the home. He will be a more dutiful father than those of any other sign. You may need to help him to enjoy his children and not take his duties so seriously that he misses the pleasures of being a parent. If he feels he is not a good father he may become very morose.

CAPRICORN CO-WORKERS

Like the tough little goat which is his symbol, the Capricorn finds many obstacles as he struggles toward his goals. His job, any job, must lead to a higher rung and he will labor tenaciously to get there in his particular field. Because he has good reasoning ability and ambition, he may likely become an executive. He does not expect to remain a co-worker for long. He is not flashy or "pushy," simply coldly determined to get where he is going. Other co-workers who impose on him find that he can be quite unexpectedly cold and ruthless. This surprises people who have typecast him in his accustomed role as "Mr. Nice Guy." His job is very important to him for many reasons. Capricorns are always thinking ahead to that rainy day or to their retirement and they know it is going to require money.

Your Capricorn co-worker is very conscientious, sometimes to a fault. He comes in early and leaves a few minutes late.

When office routine becomes unglued, Capricorn loves to help sort it out. Bosses, astute ones, call on him to detour through the confusion to the heart of the problem. He has a quiet ability to perform well under stress. He is especially adept at dealing with officials who may be able to wield some authority. Local politicians, militant citizen committees, even IRS representatives are not able to intimidate him. They represent a challenge, and he deals with challenges every day of his life. However, since he reveres tradition and propriety, he will deal with his adversaries with such charm and good manners that he does not offend. The militant citizens ad hoc committee may end by modifying their demands and agreeing to work out a reasonable compromise. The IRS man may be very surprised and respectful after he has been closeted with the methodical goat and his painstakingly accurate records. He is hard to resist. All this brinksmanship is accomplished, you guessed it, in a very low key manner.

When the Capricorn deals with women he is unfailingly courteous in an old world way. He will be the one in the meeting who lights the woman's cigarettes, fetches glasses of water, etc. Sometimes in an effort to be jovial and entertaining he may tell off-color jokes. They fall flat. Its as if he tried to assume a role that is uncomfortable and he slips back into his old somber, taciturn self.

Capricorns usually don't like to travel on business, and seldom for pleasure. Traveling entails too much confusion and upsets their orderly lives. One Capricorn literally broke out into a nervous rash when he had to travel for his company. The backs of his hands itched persistently until he was safely back in his own office. He was too clever to refuse to travel because he knew it was essential to his particular job. Soon he managed to do considerably less traveling and still fulfill his responsibilities. Predictably, he was promoted to an executive position and assigns others to do the traveling.

The female Capricorn co-worker is very like her male counterpart. She is first of all a LADY. Her goals of security, authority, respect and position can be satisfied in an office as well as at home. She may end up marrying the boss because she can be as helpless as a teddy bear needing protection in the jungle. She will never sacrifice marriage for a career, but neither will she be averse to working to help the family finances. Actually, she is quite well organized and efficient whether she is working at home or in an office. She is not nearly so stable and serene as she looks. She, too, is subject to the dark, gloomy Saturn moods. She secretly fears she is inadequate, fears the past, the present or the future, or that she is unappreciated. Also, neither she nor the male Capricorn should ever be made the butt of office teasing. They are made acutely uncomfortable and simply cannot see the joke. Praise them when you can, their tender, lonely hearts will melt.

The Capricorn female co-worker will not raise her voice or spend time gossiping with the other girls because she has better things to do. She can deal with difficult persons and can be quietly persuasive. Her voice will be even and soothing and there is a gentleness in the velvet glove that persuades and flatters. A lady Capricorn in a very busy office whose job is to deal with difficult people all day and who, despite the tension and stress, presents a picture of serene composure, is typical of the Capricorn woman regardless of her background or education. Her clothing will probably be of good cut and fabric. Capricorns are very fussy about cleanliness in personal appearance. Her hems will be even and her shoes polished. Her hairdo, while maybe not the latest style, will be neat and well done, every hair in place. Capricorn women tend to have rather lifeless brown hair, somewhat lank, probably worn in the same style for many years.

Lunch hours may be spent in expensive stores searching for clothing on sale. If she can't find a good sale she may sigh, make do with what she has, wear it out or do without.

Your Capricorn co-worker, male or female, may be contributing to the support of an elderly relative. Duty is very important and not helping an aged needy relative would be unthinkable to a Capricorn.

When contributions are collected in your office, look for the leader in the charitable cause. Capricorns are great committee workers, especially for artistic benefits, the down and outers, and the defenseless. She will be more involved in group charitable efforts than in one-to-one relationships.

Both Capricorn men and women seem to grow more youthful as they grow older. Frequently little Capricorn babies look like little old men and women and then grow more youthful until they astonish you with smooth skin, snapping blue eyes at the age of seventy or more. Most Capricorns have very delicate skin and are sometimes subject to allergies to cosmetic products. Many of them do not tan very well and appear rather blotchy after a day at the beach. If you try guessing the age of some of the older Capricorn office employees you may be surprised to find they are older than they appear.

Often men and women goats relax on weekends with a hobby which is almost another vocation. Some of them are surprisingly talented and are in some type of artistic endeavor. They have an affinity for art. However, you seldom hear much about this at the office, they are, after all, supposed to be working at the office, not visiting.

CAPRICORN BOSSES

Bosses are pretty much like employees. Their qualities are emphasized. The Capricorn boss became a boss because he was orderly, conscientious and dependable. He expects his employees to be orderly, conscientious and dependable. If they are ambitious, that is their problem. As long as they play by the rules in his big office family, they will be rewarded for good behavior and disciplined for unacceptable behavior. Employees who are prone to linger by the water cooler or take long coffee breaks can expect to see their Capricorn boss materialize like a vengefull wraith when they least expect it. He expects a day's work for a day's pay. Failure to follow orders and gross stupidity send him into a frenzy. He does not bellow and storm like Taurus or Leo, but his employees know he is angry. He is more like a friendly, dignified elder statesman when furious, and manages to be well mannered even when angry.

He is a stern father to his employees, but he can also be helpful when necessary, such as when his secretary's mother is ill and she needs a loan for a short time. He will lend an understanding ear to problems, and will expect you to follow his carefully thought out advice.

Female Capricorn bosses are scarcely distinguishable from the male as she plows steadily on her special mountain. Nothing interferes with her compulsion to reach the top. She realizes this takes organization, single-minded dedication to prove herself in a man's world, but she has probably been practicing at this since babyhood. Even infant Capricorns exhibit this single-mindedness. They don't throw temper tantrums or scream or shout, but they do manage to convey their displeasure. Then they wait quietly for your answer. If it is no, they subtly wear down your resistance until you realize that you have given in, which is what they knew you would do all along. The adult female Capricorn brings with her the habit of persuasion, thoroughness and responsibility which she has been projecting all her life. You will not see her polishing her nails or going to the beauty shop on office time. She will manage her personal life so that it does not interfere with her office duties. At the same time, as with her male counterpart, you will not see her being wishy-washy or sentimental in her executive position. Her employees will respect her authority or they may find themselves looking for another job. This also applies to many employees who make the mistake of being too friendly with her. A gauche remark delivered in front of business associates may well relegate the tactless one to future oblivion.

Employees who expect to be complimented on their work had better look to other bosses, such as Cancers. Compliments, whether from or to him, reduce him to silent embarassment and he feels at a loss for words. The most an employee may get for a compliment is a gruff "not bad" or "that's okay." If you give him a compliment you may see his ears getting pink but he may not indicate that he ever heard you.

Occasionally he will retreat into a deep black Saturnine gloom and seem unable to function. His office door will be closed and he will be out to office staff and callers. This is obviously not the time for well-meant interfering cheerfulness from his employees; he will recover when and as he can. Capricorns are remarkably psychic and experience some rather prophetic dreams when they are in the throes of depression. For example, Abraham Lincoln suffered deep depressions which almost immobilized him. Shortly before his death at the hands of assassin John Wilkes Booth, Lincoln dreamed he had been shot and his body was lying in state in the East Room of the White House. His dream, which he mentioned to associates and to his wife, closely tallied with his death and the official ceremonies which followed. Remember the strength of Capricorn; the ability to utililize, conserve, crystallize, persevere, concentrate, cling, organize. The nature of Capricorn has been described by Ronald C. Davidson, well known astrology writer. He cites the negative side of the Capricorn nature as austere, severe, snobbish uninspired. He notes that Capricorns need to cultivate sociability, buoyancy and effective self-expression in order to make their lives more well rounded.

Richard Nixon is a tragic example of a Capricorn. Pictures of him prior to the holocaust of Watergate clearly show signs of suffering, disappointments and melancholia. Consider the struggle Nixon waged from childhood as he literally pulled himself up by his boot straps. From a life of grinding poverty, he was able to educate himself and earn the attention of powerful men. His early failures in politics, his defeat for the Presidency by a slim margin, only served to crystallize his ambition. His eventual success in achieving the White House was shattered as he watched his carefully made world being destroyed. Remember, it is devastating for Capricorns to have to suddenly revamp their lives. Nixon was left with the soul-searing knowledge that not only had he failed, disgraced himself, he had lost that most important image to a Capricorn, INTEGRITY. Some of Nixon's public utterances reflected his terrible concern with how he would appear to historians. One felt that he was hoping against hope that somehow he would be vindicated in the years to come.

You are probably saying, Nixon brought this on himself. True. The irony seems to be that some of the other astrological signs, notably Sagittarius for example, have the benefit of its ruling Planet Jupiter, the planet of luck. Jupiter bestows upon Sagittarius prophetic inspiration and optimism and frequently rescues Sagittarians from the results of their own folly. Capricorn, ruled by Saturn, the planet of pessimisn, imparts pessimism, shyness and secretiveness, and frequently is plagued by false friends. For this reason, many Capricorns do not have many close friends although they cultivate many people who can assist them in their climb to success.

In spite of their misfortunes and disappointments, most Capricorns somehow seem to rise like a Phoenix from the ashes of their broken dreams.

As for you, working for your Capricorn boss in a less exalted position, you could do a lot worse. Capricorn bosses tend to cultivate successful people, and successful people carry a sexy charisma. If you are a female employee buzzing cheerfully, competently and charmingly about your office, working for Uncle Capricorn, you just may bump into a delightful relationship that could change your life in the wink of an eye. Since Capricorn is on his way up you will see affluent people in his office who will be quite different from the customers and associates you might find in the office of an Aquarian, who seldom likes working an office, let alone becoming executive; or in the office of a dreamy, casual Piscean. If you are cherishing some secret dream to marry and devote yourself to housewifely duties and civic projects without having to hold down your present nine-to-five job, the Capricorn office may be extraordinarily rewarding. If you already have alternate plans, your job is probably secure. At any rate, if you want to keep on working this is not to be sneezed at. Capricorn bosses are, by and large, dependable. Continue to make yourself indispensable, occasionally compliment, in an off-hand manner, lest you cause embarrassment, the one who signs your paycheck and don't let yourself become upset over occasional black moods. When the Piscean boss has packed his suitcase and headed for a scene with less responsibility and more time for creative pursuits, when the Gemini boss has used your abilities and then somehow forgotten all about you and gone on to hire another employee, the Capricorn will still be running the business, firmly ensconced in his executive authority, and paying your salary as regular as the tides.

aquarius

January 20-February 18

HIS ABLITY TO LOVE A WOMAN

Aquarius is ruled by Uranus which is the planet of originality, inspiration, dynamic self-expression, independence, will, inventiveness, eccentricity and empathy. The world is his friend. In fact you will be able to recognize him easily because of his frequent use of the word "friend." Remember Franklin Delano Roosevelt's "My Friends?" Even if your relationship ends he will undoubtedly ask you "Can't we still be friends?" People fascinate him and he goes about collecting people and dissecting them, curious to penetrate the next mystery and delving into new Uranian philosophies. A break up with you won't devastate him as a broken romance would devastate a Piscean or a Cancer. His interests are legion and you would be wise to not overreact when he puts down your ego.

How do you recognize Aquarius? Aquarius eyes are dreamy, looking into the distance and usually, but not always, hazel, gray or blue. The hair is blond, silky,fine but it could be dark brown. They are usually tall people, although as you know, the Ascendant modifies the physical appearance. Aquarian features are rather chiseled and regular. They have a peculiar habit of asking you a question and then dropping their head or cocking it to one side. This reaction is apparent even in a small Aquarian child.

There are often female characteristics in the male body and vice versa. You will see female Aquarians with broad shoulders and male Aquarians with broad hips. Uranus is the ruling planet and has a dual sexuality.

Despite their preoccupation with friendship, perversely, Aquarians do not have very many real friends. They consider themselves friends to the whole world. There is too much to discover to limit themselves to the natural obligations of maintaining solid friendships over the years. If you want to be his real friend be prepared to have your motives and your innermost thoughts questioned. He loves to ask embarrassing questions. His is the most curious sign in the Zodiac and he always wants to know what is going on. If you do become close he won't discard you because of some nasty gossip he has heard although he will listen to what others say about you. When all is said and done he makes up his own mind.

He will give you his opinion frankly but he won't tell you, ever, how you should live your life or what to eat or what to wear. He wants to do his own thing; you do yours. If your distant drummer music is different from his, your individuality will be respected. The Aquarian philosophy is that each person should be himself and have the freedom to experiment and express. Does this philosophy sound familiar to you? The world is now moving into the Aquarian age. On every side we see examples of new and revived sects and leaders who preach equality, brotherhood, love for all, meditation, vegetarian diets, health fads, nudity, female liberation and equal rights for minority groups. These are all Aquarian values.

Your Aquarian does not enjoy loneliness but there is a rather impersonal tone in his relationships with women. He is really looking for a companion and a friend. When he sees the woman he wants he lets her know immediately. He is not at all devious.

For years you may have known an Aquarian as a good friend and suddenly he becomes your lover. To appeal to him you should read the following homework and consider it well, or you may wind up sadly disillusioned. You could become the ex-wife, an unhappy state I trust you are not planning at this time. This man is extremely complex.

Your Aquarian has many many friends who need him as much as you do. He has the rare gift of accepting another person just as he is with all his faults and virtues. He allows his friends the marvelous freedom of being themselves with no pretenses. He is able to do this from the fullness of his heart because he is able to love all humanity. This relationship is an evolution of the fellowship of Gemini and the partnership of Libra. He is able to give the best that is within him without demanding anything in return.

He may love you as dearly as he can love any one person, but that does not mean he has ceased to love all humanity. You must, of necesssity, learn to share him with all his other friends and also with any ideas which possess him.

If you can manage to capture his undivided attention so that he is concentrating on your alone, he will be a free and uninhibited lover. He will tell you his sexual fantasies you want you tell him yours. He will want to try all sorts of experiences with you just to see if it can be done. He is intellectually curious. He wants to know why, to learn and to investigate. He will even be interested in your makeup and may even want you to experiment with different shades of eye shadow just to see how they would look. If he thinks you are as intellectually oriented as he and more interested in ideas than most women he has dated, he will begin to consider you seriously.

He is not really a cold person, but his approach is not an emotional one and he makes decisions by evaluating facts and from observations. He is rather an unconventional man and likely to embrace the avantgarde.

Sometimes he may decide that the world owes him a living. With his Aquarian love of the ideal he may fail to see that he is being unrealistic and stubborn. Even though his idea is compassionate, progressive and prophetic, its lack of acceptance may crush him; the world is just not ready for this reasoning. He is apt to be considered an eccentric in light of this pattern. He will probably always be ahead of his time.

Actually, part of his view of the future has to do with domestic serenity and harmonious relationships in the family. This is where you come in. Although he does not have any strong ambitions toward marriage, once he finds a woman who offers him intellectual and spiritual companionship he becomes a good husband. When he finds such a woman he will remain faithful and constant to her.

RELATIVES

As you might expect, he has no really close feeling for his relatives just because they are relatives. He will help them financially but then, he helps everyone who needs it. He will seek their company if they are interesting and stimulating people; otherwise he will turn to his friends. He is not at all interested in big Christmas or Thanksgiving parties just for the sake of family ties.

MONEY AND CAREER

Generally, this man is not a money-maker. In fact, he is so unworldly that he may give away his last cent to someone he thinks needs help. His solar second house is Pisces, his eighth house is Virgo. There can be exceptions of course, but if you are looking for a safe, affluent home you are better advised to concentrate on the corporation image Capricorn or the go-getter Scorpio. Your Aquarian may have a dreadful credit rating, for whatever that is worth to you.

In a profession such as medicine, law, engineering, or education, he will do very well as long as he can deal with abstract ideas. As a public health doctor he would be tops! He would be a fascinating lecturer on almost any subject. If he is a trial lawyer he will give his all to win a case for the underdog. Any profession that calls for broad, altruistic planning is his forte.

Sales work is rather a stopgap until something else comes along. He likes to deal wtih groups of people and does not do too well on a one-to-one relationship. Manual labor is anathema. He needs to get into a position where he can use his abilities to direct other people. If he has his own business he needs a partner who will protect him from erratic decisions that may ruin him. He will probably do very well selling a service or product without actually handling it. He would be superb at devising ideas for company fringe benefits or new methods of dealing with employee organizations.

HEALTH AND DIET

Aquarians are prone to illnesses connected with the circulatory system. They react poorly to heat and cold. Many pass away with heart disease because of hardening of the arteries. Their legs and ankles are weak points and they have frequent sore throats. If sore throats are diagnosed as severe it may mean a later attack of rheumatic fever. Aquarians think so rapidly, despite their appearance of dreaminess, their nervous systems are usually keyed up. This sometimes keeps them from getting enough sleep. They have difficulty "turning off" their active inquisitive minds long enough to get sleep. Frequently when they do get to sleep they have disturbing dreams.

Your Aquarian friend will probably not like active sports. Walking around a golf course after an elusive little white ball? You have got to be kidding. His kid moves rapidly, but he does not. In fact, its difficult to prod him into moving fast for any reason. Sports to him are only a tremendous waste of time. You may find an occasional rare specimen who rode a bicycle in his youth and continues the sport. He will be much more likely to continue this form of exercise if it leads him to an out of the way spot about which he is curious. Maybe he heard there were rare fossils in that area or a particularly beautiful waterfall.

Uranus is the planet of sudden upsets and changes, and true to their Uranian heritage, their illnesses are sudden and unplanned. Aquarian Clark Gable who died of an unexpected heart attack, Jimmy Dean who met an early and violent death, are examples that bear this out. This doesn't mean you need to fear the imminent departure of your favorite Aquarian, it only means that his illnesses will be more unexpected than those of other signs.

FRIENDS AND SOCIAL LIFE

He likes large social gatherings, but not if the people are die hard conformists. He is not comfortable with overly conservative people. They depress him. Keep him away from your Capricorn father. He is very sociable and outgoing with people he likes. His genial and relaxed manner easily wins many friends for him. He is essentially unselfish and helpful and his friends know that they can count on him. He has the knack of making people feel as if they had known him for years. He is a very perceptive man.

Sometimes he retreats and you can't find him. He simply wants to be alone for a while but that doesn't mean to imply he is a hermit. He will be back, bright-eyed and curious, ready to see what has been going on in his absence. He really lives in the future and only visits back here with the rest of us.

CLOTHES HE LIKES TO SEE YOU WEAR

Aquarius will be intrigued by all your clothing and he especially likes odd color combinations and accessories. He will have suggestions about all of this—listen to him, for he will come up with ideas that never occurred to you and they will work.

HOW TO ENTERTAIN AN AQUARIAN

If you are the instigator of the first date, it might be more diplomatic to avoid a quiet supper alone. Instead you should plan some interesting activity. If he still attracts you after your initial encounter, then the two of you might enjoy being alone together. Remember how much an Aquarian enjoys people so don't overreact if he includes his friends in your outings together.

Aquarians are the experimenters of the zodiac. Has he ever tried hang gliding? Piloting a sail plane? Crewing on a sailboat? Zen? Visiting a museum of science and industry? Visiting a planetarium? A new musical? A play with controversial social issues? A rainmaker? Art exhibition? Nuclear power plant? A glass blower? An architectural exhibition of the house of the future? A new car show? An antique car show? If you don't happen to have access to some of these activities but you think one of them might interest him, check out your friends for help in the matter. If you have a friend that could give him any sort of behind the scenes tour, he would love it. He is a very curious man, remember? If none of the above sound right, how about sports, for the more active Aquarian, such as jogging or tennis? Is there a decidedly non-conformist community activity you would like to know more about? Your Aquarian would love to help you investigate it.

Food usually isn't as important to Aquarians as what he is doing at the moment. However, everybody has to eat once in a while and he will eventually get hungry. Wait until you see that he is running down and then invite him home with you. This supper menu might suit him. You could either barbecue the ham on a grill or bake it in the oven. The rest of the menu you will have prepared before.

Macaroni and Cheese Salad
Relishes
Hawaiian Ham Slices
Dilly French Loaf
Caramel Frosted Bars
Fresh Fruit

Add any exotic different drink you can think of that won't poison him. Surprise him.

Marinate the ham slices in a mixture of pineapple juice, soy sauce, ginger and garlic about thirty minutes. (You can do this while the barbecue is getting hot.) Grill about two minutes on each side, Heat pineapple slices on grill and serve on top of ham.

For the macaroni salad, cook the macaroni and add sliced celery, shredded carrot, chopped onion, salad oil, vinegar, mustard, Worcestershire sauce, sugar and a can of cheddar cheese soup. Chill well. (You can do this before you leave the house.)

For the Dilly French Loaf, stir together butter or margarine with about one half teaspoon of dillweed and spread between slices cut not quite through a loaf of French bread. Wrap the loaf in heavy foil and heat for twenty to thirty minutes on a grill over low coals turning frequently. (Do this before you grill the ham and pineapple slices.)

The caramel frosted bars you can buy from the bakery or make them from a cookie mix. Just add chopped almonds toasted with caramel frosting. Do these way ahead of time.

The idea is to have as much of this done ahead of time as possible and make the entire meal appear magically with no help from him. He will think you are very clever. He might just think you are interesting enough to check out further.

FOODS THAT GRATIFY HIM

You will be amazed at your Aquarian's lack of concern for food, unless you are another Aquarian. Most of the time he seems to live on air. You can tempt his appetite with gourmet dishes of very subtle tastes. If you can seem to make food appear magically without fuss so much the better. At times he can be a connoisseur of good food and he will often notice the wines and comment on their heritage.

WHAT KIND OF HUSBAND WILL HE BE?

He will expect his home to be comfortable, a place where he can be himself. There will be a lot of emphasis on books and music. If you enjoy his tastes so much the better. He will, however, give you freedom to be yourself. Most of all he wants a companion and a friend. He does not want to journey through life alone; he abhors loneliness. He is a passionate man and you must express your love daily with him. Share his enthusiasms and your marriage will remain a living and growing companionship. He will exhibit some of the Leo characteristics such as the dramatic poise and leadership you have noticed in your Leo men. He will enjoy giving parties for his many friends.

Make sure you don't cling to him or he will feel trapped. Keep up on the current books and news events so you don't bore him. Don't let the details of running the home interfere with your life together. Don't expect him to deal with leaky faucets; he has neither the talent nor the inclination.

WHAT KIND OF FATHER WILL HE BE?

He will emphasize education for his children and will spare no effort to see that they have intellectual stimulation in the home. He has accumulated a vast store of knowledge and will fascinate them with his variety of interests. He will command their respect because of his intelligent guidance. He will treat his children with great affection but he will not overwhelm them with sentimentality. He will endeavor to create mutual appreciation because he knows this will endure long after the emotional trivia is spent. When his children leave the home he will not cling to them but will remain their true and faithful friend.

AQUARIAN CO-WORKERS

Aquarians are not indigenous to offices so you may have some difficulty finding one in yours. They frequently rocket around from office to office and then leave to go into business for themselves. He may be a clown, a disc jockey, historic researcher or an authority on whales. He might be a bush pilot in Alaska. The dull daily routine is not for him. When he does find a vocation he likes he will stay there for a lifetime.

If you do find an Aquarian in your office he will be a conscientious worker as long as he stays. He can soak up office procedures and knowledge almost by osmosis and startle his superiors with a grasp of his duties much faster than was expected.

As an example, a male Uranian employee competed in an examination taken by about fifteen hundred applicants. He was one of twelve appointed to a very desirable civil service job. His previous careers included real estate, banking, and at one time he was a yacht broker. He had a strong scientific bent and a sincere interest in people. The job to which he was appointed involved working with people. He wrote brilliant reports that were fair and unbiased. He did not allow his emotions to color his judgment. This is typical of the sign.

Neither male nor female Aquarians will make friends to the exclusion of others in the office. Any attempt on the part of their co-workers to organize them into cliques will be doomed to failure. An Aquarian doesn't like to get tied down—there is too much to investigate in this world.

Both men and women will be courteous. Both will probably wear unusual combinations of fabrics and colors. A female Aquarian will mix her granny dress with clunky shoes and toss over her shoulders a shawl that she found at Goodwill. Typical is the behavior of a woman who was enjoying a coffeebreak at the office and listening to a discussion of the stock market when suddenly she said, "Did you know that the Eskimos are going to get a welfare grant?" One of her Taurean co-workers described this nonsequitor as similar to a phonograph record which suddenly skipped a groove. When she did this frequently the Taurean would say, "Whoops, she's skipping a groove again!"

Aquarian women are by turns timid, then rowdy. At times she will be rather shy, then the Uranian influence breaks through and her mood changes like lightning. Any attempts by chauvinistic male co-workers to put them down will result in their becoming as approachable as a Russian ambassador. She is there, but she isn't.

Aquarians do not bite and claw their way to the top. However, since they are so bright and talented a wise boss may promote them and thereby put the firm on the front pages. Aquarius will give a full day's work for a day's pay and he is realistic about his own worth. Money is not the driving force for him that it is to a Capricorn or Cancer. In fact, as long as he has enough to meet his needs he can live in a garret or a posh apartment, it doesn't matter which one.

AQUARIAN BOSSES

If Aquarian employees are rather rare, Aquarian bosses are almost nonexistent. If you have checked your bosses' vital statistics thoroughly and he still comes out Aquarian, you do indeed have a rare specimen. Aquarians do not like RESPONSIBILITY, GIVING ORDERS, STAFF MEETINGS, COMMITTEE MEETINGS. If he does by some miracle find himself an executive the Uranus pops up and he rises to the challenge. He deals with the immediate situation in his own imaginative manner, never mind that nobody ever did that before, and presto, his employees are scratching their heads and remarking why they didn't think of that. If he puts his mind to it he can be a very competent boss in spite of those far away eyes and the bumbling professor image. Underneath that rumpled head of hair there is a sharp-witted mind. Remember what we said about Uranian intuitiveness? Add that to his bag of tricks and you have a more than competent executive.

This man can pick up vibrations out of the air that tell him what is going on in every corner of the office. While he ambles casually around chatting with this person or that, you can feel the wheels clicking around in his head.

He expects honesty in his staff. He is astounded when he finds an emplyee who lacks that quality.

The Aquarian office will be casual and friendly. You need to be on the look-out for surprises, though, such as coming back from your vacation to find your office has been moved two floors away. He forgot to tell you. Or your day off has been changed from Sunday to Monday. He forgot to tell you again. This brings up a peculiar quirk of Uranian character. When he does tell you something, listen very carefully the first time. You had better understand it the first time he tells you.

We talked about Capricorn giving advice to his office family and how he takes the time to give thought to the problem. His employees are expected to take his advice. Not true with the Aquarian boss. He will neither listen to you nor advise you if you ask him. So what if your kid sister smokes pot. If you linger too long at the Friday happy hour in the bar frequented by your company and consequently make a perfect ass of yourself, he will probably go so far as to defend you. You were doing your own thing on your own time. Nor will he object if the office boy wears his long locks in a pony tail tied with a string. But that office boy better do his job efficiently. No one in an Aquarian office has time to relax; there is too much going on.

Dishonest, lazy and compulsively rigid personalities just don't fit in and are soon replaced by honest, energetic and flexible employees. It is quite an interesting place to work.

pisces
February 19-March 20

HIS ABILITY TO LOVE A WOMAN

Pisces is the sign of the fish, actually, two fish, each swimming in a different direction. It is the most mystical and occult of all the signs.

Your Pisces man is idealistic and secretly doubts if he will ever find his true soul mate, but he keeps on looking.

He is a very loving and sentimental man. He can be moved to tears by the sight of children or animals in distress. He will do almost anything for a friend or a lover. He rather likes to lean on other people.

Since he is so sensitive, he frequently finds himself in a situation where he may realize that he has been imposed upon and used, perhaps over a long time. Then he blows up. But sometimes his timing is off; he blows up after a situation has existed. If he becomes angry at you, take a little time and try to puzzle out what made him react as he did. You may both be surprised at his real reasons; an event that occured some time ago.

You can be a very moody man and don't be upset if he doesn't call you for a whole weekend and later tells you he spent the time in his room thinking. When he has given of himself for a long period of time he feels emotionally drained and he needs to get off by himself to meditate. He has so much to give and to receive.

Your Pisces man has unusual eyes. They are wide and dreamy and seem to look through you, away, and then beyond you. He seldom gazes directly at you. Some Pisces eyes are really beautiful and full of strange lights. Sometimes they are slightly protruding and extremely compelling. The features are classic and expressive and the skin is smooth and free of wrinkles.

The hair usually is fine and wavy. Sometimes it is dark but most Pisceans have light hair. Oddly, the hands are either very large and ham-like or small and fragile. The feet can be small even in male Pisceans, or else rather large, tired looking and spread out. They seem to go to one extreme or the other. Most Pisces are of average height. Leos glide when they walk, Pisceans flow.

He will enjoy making love to you for hours on end. He may like to shower with you. Pisces is the watery sign. He dearly loves water in all forms: ice, pop and booze. However, he seems unable to handle alcohol well and this is a sign that can easily become an alcoholic. Very few Pisceans can stop at one social cocktail and then leave it alone.

At their best, Pisceans are idealistic and at their worst, drifters. They are not individualists; in fact seem hardly aware of their own individual talents. They are gentle, shy, super sensitive and prone to melancholy. Whereas Capricorns suffer for awhile and then the goat gets up and plods along, not so the fish. Many artists are born under this sign and quite a few have had tragic careers. The dramatic and unconventional Nijinsky had Pisces rising. The pessimistic German philosopher Schopenhauer was born under Pisces with Saturn very prominent in his horoscope. Chopin was another Piscean whose talent was obscured by an early death.

According to some Hindu authorities Pisces has reached the zenith of Yoga or spiritual consciousness, the top of the zodiacal ladder. Some mystics refer to an "old soul," meaning a person who has lived many lifetimes before on earth. They think that somehow the soul can choose each lifetime and those who have chosen the most difficult of all lives to live are Pisceans. The Piscean is supposed, according to these mystics, to have combined all the advantages and adversities of the other eleven signs. He has the trait of Virgo in that he can organize details. He loves pleasure like a Libran. He combines the sympathy and crankiness of Cancer. Sometimes he can be as brutally outspoken as a Sagittarius or as funny as Leo, as devoted to duty as a Capricorn. He likes to tease and analyze like an Aquarian. He can fly around like Gemini, be as placid as Taurus, and has the keen perception of Scorpio without the Scorpion brutality. A fascinating and complex mixture is this sign.

Pisces is a water sign but he loves to argue as do the air signs and has the love of all outdoors in common with the earth signs. He also has the unique power of being able to telescope his past, present and future into his vision of the moment.

Since the fish is always suffering with humanity and has so much empahty for others he tries to conceal this trait. To do this he is sometimes witty and funny or brittle and merciless. Whatever his mood, it is his way to cover up. He simply can't be spontaneous. He has found out the hard way how vulnerable he can be to other people's rage. He sometimes develops this self-protection into an art and as a result some fish are tremendously gifted actors and actresses. They seem to know the word, the gesture, the inflection to provoke the desired reaction from their audience. This brings up another little quirk you may find difficult to cope with. The Piscean, somewhat like Gemini, will hardly ever be truthful with you all the time. For some obscure reason he may tell you he stopped at the grocery or the hardware store to pick something up and they were out of it. He probably wasn't anywhere near the hardware store or the grocery store and went for a walk. He finds it easier to tell you a fib than simply say, "I wanted to be alone for a while." If you do discover the truth, let it go at that. He can't help it. He also can't help being gregarious and many friends with problems will call him, sometimes at all hours. He is so sympathetic. If you overreact in a situation like this you can create problems for yourself. He isn't immune to pretty legs or a lovely face because he does admire beauty, but he really isn't wolfish either. Your biggest problem, aside from financial ones, will be his tendency to fall into the glooms. Then you had better cheer him up. He is quite prone to suggestion and you will have to discover for yourself what works best with your man. If you leave him to his own devices he may stay remote and depressed for quite some time. Pisces does have a streak of self-destructiveness. Psychiatrists describe people like this as "picking at their scabs." Pisces tends to dwell on his hurts. He is hurt if he is not invited to the party and hurt if he is. You can cope with this more effectively if you are matter of fact and get him up and moving to get his mind off his difficulties. You can perk him up with a delightful surprise all planned by you. Tickets for a show perhaps, or a sporting event; maybe a boat race. He does enjoy water sports and may even own his own boat. Sometimes he is simply tired, what with the demands of earning a living and soaking up the problems and activities of his friends.

Typical is a Pisces who loves the water and has a boat. This fellow is rather taciturn until he knows someone well enough to open up and communicate. He is extremely perceptive and kindly. He works full time but always finds the hours to enjoy his boat because it can take him away from civilization and allow him to recharge his energies. People simply wear him out after a while and he has found this escape.

Pisces will take great pains selecting gifts for you. You can crush him by rejecting his gifts. He will be eager to please you and deeply hurt if he thinks he hasn't succeeded.

Whatever you do, don't take advantage of him. This is the story of his life. People are always taking advantage of Pisces because he is so self-sacrificing.

He is not a very verbal lover but he does like to be touched and petted. He will reward you by showing you thoughtfulness and tenderness you never expected to find in any man. He will identify with your deepest emotions and you will never have to explain your moods to him. He will simply *know*. Your friends will probably tell you he is the most understanding man they have ever met, which may be true. If you work in an office the man who picks up the get well card and flowers for the sickbed employee is probably a Pisces.

RELATIVES

Pisces can be imposed upon by his relatives. Your middle-aged date who frequently stays at home to care for his aged mother is very likely a Pisces. He can fall into a trap because it is so hard for him to take a stand against injustice.

MONEY AND CAREER

Money per se is not too important to Pisces. He isn't very practical about paying his bills and frequently gets into difficulty because he lets financial matters slide.

Actually your Pisces man has a great deal of initiative if he would only use it. It is very hard for him to face up to any unpleasant situation. He usually solves the matter by simply retreating. It is all just too painful. On the other side of the coin he can be a very proud man who doesn't want to be beholden to anyone. If he finds that he can't get by on his income he will probably start a side line rather than ask his boss for a raise. He has more ambition that he realizes and sometimes becomes a success accidentally.

He has a special talent for handling real estate. If he finds himself in a profession such as medicine, law, engineering, education, social work or the ministry he will be very successful. Many talented beauticians are Pisces. His quiet charming personality will attract people to him. Internal medicine and psychiatry are especially good fields for him. People invariably confide their troubles to him and these fields allow him to utilize his gifts for empathy and intuition.

Your Pisces man may be a very successful veterinarian, because he loves animals. He will also be a good salesman, but not because he high-pressures his customers into buying his product. He is such a good listener and so adept at drawing people out that they sell themselves. As a sales manager he may have mixed success. He has great intuition regarding buying trends but he doesn't make a good executive because it is hard for him to give orders. It is painful to the point of illness for him to have to discharge an unsuccessful employee. He dislikes responsibility and when it is unavoidable, he worries about it.

He could be a fine actor or dancer because he is able to make his characterizations live and breathe reality.

He tends to worry even when he doesn't have a valid reason for worrying. He has difficulty about making decisions becaue he doesn't trust himself to make the right decision. He doesn't operate very well or happily in partnerships because he worries about what his partner is doing.

If he can become motivated enough to stop being so irresponsible and dreamy he can become one of the world's workers. Pisces, of all the signs, most needs financial security. He can then become less defensive and more spontaneous when he isn't eternally plagued by the worry about money.

HEALTH AND DIET

Pisces is not very strong and his muscles are small. He seems to have too much fluid in his body. He needs a schedule of regular meals and mild exercise. Sometimes he gets bored and depressed and imagines that he is ill. Narcotics, liquor and drugs are bad for him. If he has someone to love him and the proper food and relaxation he will be healthy and happy. Too much sleep isn't good for him; he can indulge in unreal fantasies. He needs to be reminded that there is a real world out there. Frequently Pisces doesn't take very good care of himself physically. He seems to think he can live forever. Since he is so involved in helping out friends and relatives, he may function on his nervous energy. This can be a severe drain on him, and he really isn't terribly strong to start with.

Pisces suffers from accidents involving the feet, hands, hips, and they catch colds and flu that sometimes develop into pneumonia. They have either very strong feet or weak arches and ankles. They love to psyche themselves either into or out of illnesses or moods.

FRIENDS AND SOCIAL LIFE

He has many friends who are attracted to him because he is a gentle and compassionate friend. If he can control his tendency to become suspicious without cause he can keep his friends. He has difficulty being himself with his friends, and frequently he tries too hard and defeats himself. Often, too, he is so self-centered he is not really listening to his friend; he is listening to himself and evaluating how well he is going over.

CLOTHES HE LIKES YOU TO WEAR

He would rather not see you in any clothes. If you must dress to go out with him try wearing grays, blue-greens and orchids. He likes soft, sheer dresses, the color of the sea. He enjoys seeing girls with long, flowing hair. Magnolia, Lilac and Lilly of the Valley perfumes turn him on.

HOW TO ENTERTAIN YOUR PISCEAN

First of all, try to determine his mood or estimate what his mood will probably be when you do entertain him. If he has had a hard week, try to unwind him over the weekend. You want him to find relaxation and relief with you if other people have been dropping their problems in his lap all week. You may have to keep your plans flexible. Usually, if he is a typical fish and does not have a strong Cancer ascendant to keep him home, he likes to travel. He may want to sail off in his boat, fly off in his plane to find a fun resort that is a real change from his normal work day world. Go with him.

If he is feeling social, try a beach picnic. Plan to have hot dogs or steaks or a fish fry. If he just wants to enjoy your tasty home cooking the following might be in order:

Tossed Green Salad with Tomatoes
and Mild Dressing
Roast Chicken with Bland Stuffing
Potatoes Au Gratin
Creamed Peas and Carrots with Savory Dressing

Cheese Cake

Serve him his favorite liquor, perhaps bourbon, scotch or a vodka drink. You may want to choose a light white wine to go with the chicken and top off the meal with a creme de menthe. Keep the seasonings subtle and delicate; he isn't too fond of highly spiced foods. Have ample portions; this man is a hearty eater. He likes to really fill up. His tastes may not be very sophisticated so don't get too exotic.

Go easy on inviting a house full of guests for a party until you find out his mood. How you entertain the fish will depend entirely on how perceptive you are—how you read him—where his head is at the moment. To be successful, be responsive and most of all, be flexible.

FOODS THAT GRATIFY HIM

Your Pisces drinks more than some of the signs and will like vodka and fruit juice. If he turns out to be a health food devotee he won't drink at all. Then he will know all about the proper diet and will tell you what he prefers. He usually likes fish, poultry, green vegetables and soups. He likes soft music and quiet atmosphere. Some fish are hard to please, perhaps because they enjoy the feeling of not being satisfied.

WHAT KIND OF HUSBAND WILL HE BE?

He is so deeply sentimental and so easily influenced by you that you won't have much difficulty marrying him. In fact, you may find it hard to get rid of him. As a married man he will cherish you and your home. He won't go looking for affairs outside of marriage. However, if it does happen it will be because he is pursued and will just drift into the relationship. He will feel so guilty he will want to come home to you so you can punish him and he can forget the whole miserable mess. He will want you to tell him it really wasn't his fault. This could very well be true.

As a wife you need to reember that you are dealing with a very sensitive individual and treat him accordingly. While the negative side of his nature is hard to understand at times he can be the most devoted of husbands. He will be extremely responsive to you sexually and this will continue long past middle age.

Your Pisces man knows that he needs a wife he can communicate with. He has problems that can best be solved by his talking with you. This helps to clarify the situation. Sometimes he will ask you for advice. When you offer it, very likely he won't take it; he only wanted you to sympathize with him.

Try not to give him too much sympathy. It tends to weaken him and adds to his tendency to become a martyr. He really is much stronger than he thinks he is; encourage him to realize his many strengths.

Love him and appreciate him for his good qualities. Try not to let his moods upset you; they aren't that important. Give him a den of his own where he can recharge his batteries. If you can discover a secluded home near the sea you will make him a very happy man.

WHAT KIND OF FATHER WILL HE BE?

As a father he will love his children but he will expect you to take care of the details of their up-bringing. He will simply enjoy them. Let him assume his natural role of confidant and companion to his children. Don't try to force him into an unnatural relationship. It would be extremely painful for him to punish a child physically, for example. Since he is such a good companion and understands his children so well there won't be much necessity for punishment. He will make the children feel loved and secure in his own way, even though he may seem rather casual about it.

PISCES CO-WORKERS

There are more employees than employers born under this sign. The quiet, sympathetic secretary who gets along with everyone on the office staff and seems to be the one people come to with their troubles is probably a Pisces. The fish has a delightful sense of humor which is never far from the surface. She is happy and contented if her boss has agreed to her request for lush green carpeting, soft green draperies. She will keep her bosses' desk and hers supplied with fresh flowers.

Fish take on the color of their surroundings and are miserable if they have to work in a dull, drab office. After a while they sort of fade away and become dull and drab too. Bright greens, yellows and ocean-like blue colors give them back their pizzazz.

Critcism makes the fish disappear. They are so super sensitive they try hard to do their work and avoid criticism. When they are criticized unfairly its as if a sword descended from the sky and their immediate reaction is to swim away. If criticism continues to rain down upon their defenseless heads they will swim away permanently. Of course, as is true of all signs, if there is a Cancer, Scorpio or Capricorn ascendant they will fight back and defend themselves vigorously. In fact, offices being what they are today, Pisces who don't have a strong ascendant probably won't survive. Pisces usually don't get fired. They quit. Ironically they often quit when they could effect a confrontation and come out ahead.

If the employee is a lady fish, she is probably only treading water until she gets married.

Neither sex will go tooth and nail after someone's job. Getting another job like this isn't worth diving into the murky depths of shark infested waters where there is the risk they could be gobbled up.

As long as they stay around the office they are reliable employees putting in overtime if necessary. They may be rather sloppy at home, but at work their desks will be neat and orderly.

You will hardly ever find a fish in an office marked "Bookkeeper." They are bewildered by the importance others place on money. Money is something to spread around wherever needed. If one of his friends needs money the Pisces will gladly lend it to him. He himself sometimes runs short and he understands this.

Social work and nursing attract Pisces. Fish love to work in amateur theatricals and love to paint scenery backstage if they do not make the tryouts. Some earn fantastic salaries as actors and actresses. Elizabeth Taylor is an example. Amateur theatricals are good for them because if they work at depressing jobs they become depressed and they suffer. Too much suffering by the empathetic Piscean is destructive to their sensitive natures. Play acting is the perfect antidote for their fears and depressions. They seem to understand this danger instinctively and maneuver themselves out of potentially threatening situations thus enabling them to avoid the annihilation of the personality. If the fish is physically unable to escape the environment that is causing such pain and sorrow he may take the only way out, escape through illness. This accounts for their occasional spells of being accident prone. However, illness and accidents are not consciously sought as a survival mechanibm.

PISCES BOSSES

A Pisces boss is about as out of place as spinach on a tooth. Bosses imply executive positions. This usually means confinement in an office, ambition to achieve, a structured environment and constant association with people who have a strong dynamic drive for success. That is the last atmosphere the fish wants. He needs room to swim around freely, strike out on his own and then sink quietly in the depths to dream over his experiences. Corporate institutions do not usually cater to this life style in the current age of intensive competition. Pisces is not particularly competitive. He sees no reason to engage in dog eat dog survival and will attempt to avoid working in that kind of arena if at all possible.

However, he does need money even if only to give it to others who happen to need it more at the time than he does. In a way he is sort of a middle man for money and it passes through his fingers rapidly, like water through a sieve.

If he is motivated enough to work, and it may take quite some time for him to get to that point, he may be drawn to travel agencies, airline companies or television studios where he can live in the make believe. He sometimes runs a dance studio, or he may be a ski instructor. Some fish are writers. Most Pisceans are born actors.

If you do have that rare harborless, nebulous specimen behind the door marked President in your office, very likely you are working in an artistically or culturally oriented field. This boss can be very creative. He also makes a good public relations man because he knows instinctively how to soften the initial brutal truth in dealing with people. He can be a very inspiring teacher. Some fish do become teachers and are beloved by their students, as the famous Mr. Chipps, for example. There is a charming Piscean teacher of the fourth grade who spends many more hours than most teachers in parent conferences. She grades the children's papers most carefully and writes little notes of encouragement on each one. She knows praise will motivate her students far more than criticism. Typical of a Pisces, she has such a tender heart she brings home stray animals and cares for them until she can find them loving homes. At present she has four dogs and a cat. She also has been to Europe twelve times on her summer vacations, sometimes with her husband and sometimes alone. Her husband understands her need to travel alone occasionally and allows her freedom.

Another beautiful dreamy eyed Piscean lived with her widowed mother and cared for her after all her brothers and sisters had left the home. She drifted from one innocuous occupation to another. Finally, much to her mother's surprise, she became an airline stewardess. She now flies happily about the country, coming home from time to time to check on her mother. She can combine her love of travel with her obligation. No doubt her passengers adore her. She caters to their wishes before they ask. However, by the time you read this she may have floated off to another career or quit entirely to walk along the seashore and dream. Neptune souls do have that need to be alone to revitalize their energies.

A peculiarity of Piscean bosses is that sometimes he can be a bit sneaky. He can make statements such as "I gave up adding to people's anxiety levels a long time ago," and the next minute do you in. He alternates between criticism and tenderness. He can argue a point from both sides and often does, like Libra. Some days he will be taciturn and other days he may chatter on for hours. You have to learn to swim with his current and not fight it. He admires and respects hard-headed employees and keeps a supply of them around the office to buffer him from the cold cruel world. If he is in a creative field he will have creative thinkers around too but if there is a business recession he is practical enough to fire the creative cloud nine thinkers and hang onto those who have been around long enough to know how to keep the company doors open. If he does have to ax an employee he will wave him a sad farewell. It is painful for him to fire anyone.

The fish boss will know if an employee is having personal problems. His radar is out there bleep-bleeping signals to his tender heart. He can be a comfort but may act gruff to make it seem casual.

His anger will show itself in sarcasm but he can't roar like Taurus. When he does get angry he surprises himself and others by being more verbal than usual. A strong jolt of anger gets rid of his inhibitions and his intelligence comes into sharp focus.

what you've always wanted to know about horoscopes

All over the world people were being born on the same day you were, but chances are few that very many were born at the same time and place as you. Thus you are unique. Your horoscope is unique.

If the sun was passing through the sign of Aries, your sun sign would be Aries. This is dependent on your time of birth. Your individual horoscope is unique also because of the particular placement of the other planets at the time of your birth. Perhaps you are an Arian and the Moon was in Leo at that time. Jupiter might have been in Capricorn or Saturn in Sagittarius. Mercury, however, never revolves far from the Sun; it will be either in your Sun sign or the one directly after it. If you want to be technical, Mercury is never more than twenty-eight degrees away from the Sun and Venus never more than forty-eight degrees. Both Venus and Mercury will always be close to any Sun sign.

The position of all these planets marks you indelibly as being the unique person you are. They influence your body, your personality and the way in which you present yourself to others.

The Moon makes a complete transit of the zodiac every twenty-seven days, seven hours and forty-three minutes, approximately. Thus the Moon is in a particular sign of the zodiac for a little over two days. The Sun, Mercury and Venus spend about a month at a time in each of the twelve signs of the zodiac.

It takes Mars twenty-two months on an average to complete its transit of the zodiac and stays in each sign about two months. Jupiter takes twelve years to travel through the zodiac, going through one sign each year. Saturn travels through the zodiac every twenty-nine and one-half years, spending about two and a half years in each sign. Uranus takes eighty-four years, Neptune one hundred and sixty-five years, and Pluto about three hundred and twenty-four years to get through the entire zodiac.

Uranus stays in one sign for seven years, Neptune stays in one sign for fourteen years and Pluto stays in one sign for twenty-seven years.

If, for example, you find your horoscope shows that Neptune was in Capricorn when you were born, it will endow you with strong reasoning powers and strong faith. If at the present time it has again entered the sign Capricorn it will be with you for another fourteen years, which will be great for you!

SUN

Each planet influences certain aspects of your life. The Sun is the greatest planet of all. The symbol for the Sun is a dot within a circle symbolizing life emerging. It is masculine and represents health, government, high office and general publicity. It has influences over prosperity, new undertakings and popularity. It designates proud or haughty persons. The day associated with the Sun is Sunday, the metal is gold, the color is orange.

MOON

For some reason to the Babylonians the Moon was male, but later it came to represent the female. It is responsible for sailors, shell fish, amphibious animals, swans, geese, seaweed, cucumber, melon and mushrooms. It obviously affects the tides and very likely menstruation. The Moon's connection with health has always made it prominent in medical astrology. Max Heindel, one of the best known American astrologers, has written papers on the best time for surgical operations, the best time he feels is when the Moon is waxing. The Greeks called the

Moon Artemis and to the Romans it was Diana.

Astrologically the Moon represents fruitfulness and rules liquids, sailing, drinking and brewing. It rules nurses and women in general. It influences people in occupations dealing with the public. Plant life is very susceptible to lunar phases.

The Moon rules the breasts, stomach, emotions and digestive functions of the body. Its day is Monday and its metal is silver. Its colors are pale yellow, silver and soft green.

MERCURY

The Romans called Mercury the messenger of the gods. The Greeks called this planet Hermes and depicted him with winged sandals and helmet. Mercury is the familiar figure for communication. Like the metal, Mercury is slippery and undependable. It is a bewildering combination, versatile and volatile at the same time. It rules ambassadors, philosophers, astrologers, teachers and in an adverse aspect, thieves. Mercury rules television, radio, radar and telephones.

Mercury is neutral, sexless, cold, dualistic. It governs travelers, speakers, clerks, printers, writers and publishers, secretaries, bookkeepers, and matters involving mailing, letters, stationery.

It rules the bowels and also the nervous system, the "messenger" of the body. Its day is Wednesday, its metal is quicksilver, its color is blue.

VENUS

The Greeks called her Aphrodite, the goddess of love and beauty. She was Venus to the Romans. In ancient Babylon she was called Ishtar, the most powerful heavenly body after the Sun and the Moon.

Venus is feminine, moist, warm, beneficial and fruitful. She rules the disposition and the sense of touch. Drama, music, painting, opera, singing, poetry and art are influenced by Venus. It is said to rule the neck, throat, kidneys and the internal reproductive system. Venus' day is Friday, its metal is copper and its colors are pink and turquoise.

MARS

The Greeks called the planet Ares and the Romans Mars, and both knew it as the warlike god. It is said to rule surgeons, military men, stockbreeders and it is felt to be malicious. Ptolemy said that Mars dries up rivers, causes crop failures. When it is setting it causes diseases and when it is rising it is responsible for injuries. It arouses anger, passions and fevers.

Mars is masculine. It is dry, hot, forceful, courageous, strong and energetic. It governs the base nature of man, his ambitions and desires, and manifests itself both constructively and destructively, depending upon its aspect. It rules chemistry, iron, steel, surgery, war and has influence over dentists, surgeons, butchers, firemen and policemen. Its day is Tuesday, its metal is iron and its color is red.

JUPITER

In Greece this planet was the god Zeus, ruler of the heavens. The Romans called him Jupiter. It is considered a lucky planet. It is masculine, moderate, social, expansive and temperate. It rules foreign service, shipping, financial enterprises and speculations. It is connected with judges, attorneys, brokers, the law, science and relativity. Jupiter rules the blood, the liver and the thighs. Its day is Thursday, its metal is tin and its color is green.

SATURN

The Greeks called him Kronos and identified him with old Father Time. He is known as the governor of old age, and is the limiting planet. When he reigns there is thought to be excessive lying, many lawsuits and endless debate. The other side of Saturn is more helpful and represents wisdom and accumulated experience.

Saturn is masculine, dry, cold, phlegmatic and melancholic. It rules masonry, bricklaying, plumbing, pottery and uncongenial occupations. It rules mines, property, real estate, coal and junk. It is said to rule the teeth, the blood circulation and the knees. Its day is Saturday and its metal is lead. Its color is black.

URANUS

The Greeks called it Ouranos. It has a glyph or symbol which looks like a television antenna. It signifies revolution, sudden and unexpected events, and typically it was discovered in 1781 about the time of the industrial revolution. It rules groups of people rather than individuals. It is associated with the age of Aquarius, for Uranus rules the zodiacal sign of Aquarius.

This planet is known to govern electricity, telegraphy, television, airplanes, dynamos, rocks and electrical appliances. It is considered malefic. It rules invention, curiosity and intuition. In the body it rules the ankles. Its metal is platinum, uranium, radium and all radioactive elements. Its color is electric blue.

NEPTUNE

The Roman god of the sea was Neptune, the same as the Greek god Poseidon. Its key words are impressionable and nebulous. Mysticism, drunkenness, emotional genius, frauds of all kinds respond to Neptune. Some astrologers connect Neptune with the sea, travel and nursing. It is the patron of mystics, psychics and mediums.
tron of mystics, psychics and mediums.

Neptune is neutral, cold, moist and can be beneficial or malicious depending upon its location in the chart. Its influence is more psychic than material or physical, and it rules secret affairs, detective work and things which are hidden or mysterious. It is thought to rule the feet and the emotions. Its metal may be tin, there is a disagreement on this point, but it rules gas, drugs, alcoholic beverages, opiates and anesthetics. Its colors are the colors of the ocean and intensified turquoise.

In astrology the Sun represents the positive life giving principle while the Moon represents the passive side. The sun rules our basic individuality. The ascendant sign rules our physical body, the way we walk and talk, our gestures and our mannerisms. The Moon rules the personality, the way we appear to others.

For example, most people have a different Sun sign, ascendant or rising sign, and a different Moon sign. While the Sun sign is generally considered to be very powerful, an individual is also influenced by the ascendant sign and the Moon. If, for example, a person's Sun is in Libra, this would make them artistically inclined. They would love beauty, peace and harmony in life. Venus is the planetary ruler of Libra so they would dislike drudgery and dirty work. Lets say the ascendant or rising sign turns out to be Aries. Aries is going to influence the physical body and the way someone walks and talks. Aries people have sharp features. Their movements are quick, their shoulders will be broad and they may walk with the head slightly bent forward. They usually seem to be in a hurry. If the Moon happens to be in Leo this will make their personality more like a Leonian. The Moon in Leo tends to make people proud and ambitious with little hesitation about assuming heavy responsibility.

These people may be very well known to the public. They are often very popular with the opposite sex and may be generous to a fault.

Of course, these are oversimplifications. There are the other planets in each chart and each will have their own influence on a person.

The Sun, Moon and ascendant are the three power points in your chart, the twelve houses are each in command of certain other aspects of personality and living. The twelve houses are ruled as follows:

First House: Physical body, self centered interests, ruler Aries.

Second House: Money, possessions and security, ruler Taurus.

Third House: Communications, relationship to environment, ruler Gemini.

Fourth House: Home, parents, beginnings and endings, ruler Cancer.

Fifth House: Children, amusements, recreation and display, ruler Leo.

Sixth House: Health, service, efficiency, ruler Virgo.

Seventh House: Partners, unity with others on a personal level, ruler Libra.

Eighth House: Sex expression, self sacrifice, ruler Scorpio.

Ninth House: Travel abroad, self projection to new horizons, ruler Sagittarius.

Tenth House   Careeer, material responsibility, social status, ruler Capricorn.

Eleventh House: Friends, hopes and wishes; identification with groups, ruler Aquarius.

Twelfth House: Self undoing, escapism, confinement, self sacrifice, ruler Pisces.

Briefly, in your chart, Jupiter acts as the planet of good fortune, and you can anticipate great results when this planet moves into the second (money) house of your chart. Keep in mind that these planets are constantly moving. When Saturn, the planet of limitations, moves into your second house you probably will have to work a little harder to make money. Saturn has been known for thousands of years and during this time billions of horoscopes were examined and compared. This planet has been shown to make people serious, profound and cautious and to inspire excellent abilities to organize and execute plans of action.

People who have Saturn in the fifth house of children, pleasure and amusement at birth tend to be deprived of these things in their lives. With Jupiter in the fifth at birth there tends to be an abundance of the things represented in that house.

These are merely brief and somewhat superficial examples of what influence the houses have and what the planets mean. Another example, Jupiter in the seventh house of partners, unity with others on a personal level, makes you social and good natured and able to enjoy beneficial partnership, prosperous and fruitful marriage, and generous and faithful partners. Jupiter in the eleventh house brings loyal friendships, sometimes with prominent people such as bankers, judges, politicians, doctors, professors, through whom you will gain social success, popularity and a good reputation. Powerful and influential friends often help you to attain ambitions and realize hopes. The eleventh house represents friends, hopes and wishes.

If you have Venus in the eighth house, the house of sex expression and self sacrifice, you will gain through business and marriage partners or inherit a legacy.

The sign of the Moon at your birth triggers certain events in your life each time the Moon completes an orbit of the earth. For instance, if your Moon is in Libra, you will be at your peak when the Moon passes through Libra.

There are only eight planets plus the Earth, Sun and Moon, but some astrologers, in order to associate one planet with each of the twelve signs, have postulated the existence of two or three additional planets. This seems confusing when you learn that the Moon rules Cancer and the Sun rules Leo. Neither the Sun nor Moon are actual planets. The ruler of a sign is which ever celestial body has characteristics most like that particular sign. Leo (Sun) people are dramatic, bold, regal. Cancer (Moon) people are sensitive and impressionable. Still, there's some kind of harmonious vibration between each heavenly body and all the signs of the zodiac. Every sign has a planetary ruler but Mercury, Venus and Mars have traditionally been assigned as the rulers of two signs each.

Mars rules Aries and Scorpio; Venus rules Taurus and Libra; Mercury rules Gemini and Virgo; the Moon rules Cancer; the Sun rules Capricorn; Uranus rules Aquarius; Neptunes rules Pisces.

Since the discovery of Pluto in 1931, this most distant planet was assigned to the sign Scorpio, leaving Mars to rule Aries only.

The Sun, Moon and ascendant in most horoscopes are usually in three different signs. There will be times, pointed out before, when a person will be born at sunrise, so his Sun sign and ascendant sign will be the same. This makes him a double of whichever Sun sign was rising. Although it is rare, there are some gifted people born during a new Moon or an eclipse who also have a whole grouping of planets in the ascending sign.

Carl Gustav June, a famous psychologist, was also a scientist. He performed an experiment using astrology that is now famous. With the usual procedure to check for and avoid any prior knowledge on the part of the investigators of the subjects, he took four hundred and eighty-three marriage horoscopes. That is a total of nine hundred and sixty-six horoscopes. He then paired off these horoscopes in different ways; he paired couples not married to each other and left other pairs intact. The object of this study was to establish the differences between the married couples and the unpaired couples. Several patterns emerged. In the married couples' horoscopes, the women's Moon appeared in conjunction with her husband's Sun more frequently. Astrologers have said that this position most favors marriage. An example of such conjunction is when two planets are close together, say eight to ten degrees of each other.

The great pioneer of astrology in the United States was Evangeline Adams (1865-1932). She was reported to be a descendant of John Quincy Adams, sixth president of the United States, which probably helped her up the ladder of success. She had a brush with the law, however, in 1914 when she was arrested in New York City for fortune telling and was given the choice of pleading guilty or paying a fine. She arrived in court armed with reference books and carefully explained how she made her predictions. She was asked to draw a horoscope for someone for whom she was given only the birthdate. By an odd coincidence this turned out to be the birthdate of the son of the judge. The judge subsequently concluded that "The defendant raises astrology to the dignity of an exact science."

People who knew Evangeline Adams described her as a very dynamic and courageous woman. She was extremely influential in making astrology "respectable." According to the American Federation of Astrologers, she was consulted by personages such as J.P. Morgan, King Edward VII, Caruso and Mary Pickford. She passed away on November 10, 1932, the date she had predicted for her own death, after having compiled some thousands of horoscopes.

During World War II the British government formed a Psychological Research Bureau. An astrologer named Louis de Wohl was commissioned with the rank of captain in the British army. He became the British government's official astrologer. De Wohl believed that Hitler employed astrologers and his task was to report to the British government what Hitler's astrologers were probably telling *him*. However, German astrologers did not fare too well in Germany during the Third Reich and many came to an unfortunate end. Hess and Himmler were thought to be advised by astrologers and one astrologer who was investigated by the Gestapo was Ernst Schulte-Strathaus. The Gestapo suspected he had something to do with Hess' sudden escape from Germany to Scotland. If there were any astrologers in good repute on Hitler's staff there seems to be little evidence that Hitler listened to them at all, that is, providing they had the courage to make accurate predictions about the eventual downfall of the Third Reich. History does record the imprisonment of one Karl Ernst Krafft and his subsequent death in the Oranienberg concentration camp on January 8, 1945.

Sidney Omarr writes in his forward to the book, *Henry Miller: His World of Urania,* in 1960:

A Science of Relating:

> Astrology does not offer an explanation of the laws of the universe, nor why the universe exists. What it does, to put it in simplest terms, is to show us that there is a correspondence between macrocosm and microcosm. In short, that there is a rhythm to the universe, and that man's own life partakes of this rhythm. For centuries men have observed and studied the nature of this correspondence.
>
> Whether astrology be a science or a pseudo-science, the fact remains that the oldest and the greatest civilizations we know of had for centuries upon centuries used it as a basis for thought and action. That it degenerated into mere fortune-telling, and why, is another story.
>
> It is not to discover what is going to 'happen' to us, it is not to forestall the blows of fate, that we should look to our horoscopes. A chart when properly read should enable one to understand the overall pattern of one's life. It should make a

man more aware of the fact that his own life obeys the same rhythmical, cyclical laws as do other natural phenomena. It should prepare him to welcome change, constant change, and to understand that there is no good or bad, but always the two together in changing degrees, and that out of what is seemingly bad can come good and vice versa. Astrology might indeed be called a science of relating, whose first fruit is the dictum that fate is character.